PHRASEBOOK

- ROMANIAN -

By Andrey Taranov

THE MOST IMPORTANT PHRASES

This phrasebook contains
the most important
phrases and questions
for basic communication
Everything you need
to survive overseas

T&P BOOKS

Phrasebook + 3000-word dictionary

English-Romanian phrasebook & topical vocabulary

By Andrey Taranov

The collection of "Everything Will Be Okay" travel phrasebooks published by T&P Books is designed for people traveling abroad for tourism and business. The phrasebooks contain what matters most - the essentials for basic communication. This is an indispensable set of phrases to "survive" while abroad.

This book also includes a small topical vocabulary that contains roughly 3,000 of the most frequently used words. Another section of the phrasebook provides a gastronomical dictionary that may help you order food at a restaurant or buy groceries at the store.

T&P Books Publishing
www.tpbooks.com

ISBN: 978-1-78492-429-4

This book is also available in E-book formats.
Please visit www.tpbooks.com or the major online bookstores.

FOREWORD

The collection of "Everything Will Be Okay" travel phrasebooks published by T&P Books is designed for people traveling abroad for tourism and business. The phrasebooks contain what matters most - the essentials for basic communication. This is an indispensable set of phrases to "survive" while abroad.

This phrasebook will help you in most cases where you need to ask something, get directions, find out how much something costs, etc. It can also resolve difficult communication situations where gestures just won't help.

This book contains a lot of phrases that have been grouped according to the most relevant topics. The edition also includes a small vocabulary that contains roughly 3,000 of the most frequently used words. Another section of the phrasebook provides a gastronomical dictionary that may help you order food at a restaurant or buy groceries at the store.

Take "Everything Will Be Okay" phrasebook with you on the road and you'll have an irreplaceable traveling companion who will help you find your way out of any situation and teach you to not fear speaking with foreigners.

TABLE OF CONTENTS

T&P Books Publishing

PRONUNCIATION

T&P phonetic alphabet	Romanian example	English example
[a]	arbust [ar'bust]	shorter than in ask
[e]	a merge [a 'merdʒe]	elm, medal
[ə]	brățară [brə'tsarə]	Schwa, rediced 'e'
[i]	impozit [im'pozit]	shorter than in feet
[ɨ]	cuvânt [ku'vɨnt]	big, America
[o]	avocat [avo'kat]	pod, John
[u]	fluture ['fluture]	book
[b]	bancă ['bankə]	baby, book
[d]	durabil [du'rabil]	day, doctor
[dʒ]	gemeni ['dʒemenʲ]	joke, general
[f]	frizer [fri'zer]	face, food
[g]	gladiolă [gladi'olə]	game, gold
[ʒ]	jucător [ʒukə'tor]	forge, pleasure
[h]	pahar [pa'har]	home, have
[k]	actor [ak'tor]	clock, kiss
[l]	clopot ['klopot]	lace, people
[m]	mobilă ['mobilə]	magic, milk
[n]	nuntă ['nuntə]	name, normal
[p]	profet [pro'fet]	pencil, private
[r]	roată [ro'atə]	rice, radio
[s]	salată [sa'latə]	city, boss
[ʃ]	cleștișor [kleʃti'ʃor]	machine, shark
[t]	statuie [sta'tue]	tourist, trip
[ts]	forță ['fortsə]	cats, tsetse fly
[tʃ]	optzeci [opt'zetʃi]	church, French
[v]	valiză [va'lizə]	very, river
[z]	zmeură ['zmeurə]	zebra, please
[j]	foios [fo'jos]	yes, New York
[ʲ]	zori [zorʲ]	palatalization sign

LIST OF ABBREVIATIONS

English abbreviations

ab.	-	about
adj	-	adjective
adv	-	adverb
anim.	-	animate
as adj	-	attributive noun used as adjective
e.g.	-	for example
etc.	-	et cetera
fam.	-	familiar
fem.	-	feminine
form.	-	formal
inanim.	-	inanimate
masc.	-	masculine
math	-	mathematics
mil.	-	military
n	-	noun
pl	-	plural
pron.	-	pronoun
sb	-	somebody
sing.	-	singular
sth	-	something
v aux	-	auxiliary verb
vi	-	intransitive verb
vi, vt	-	intransitive, transitive verb
vt	-	transitive verb

Romanian abbreviations

f	-	feminine noun
f pl	-	feminine plural
m	-	masculine noun
m pl	-	masculine plural
n	-	neuter
n pl	-	neuter plural
pl	-	plural

ROMANIAN
PHRASEBOOK

This section contains
important phrases that may
come in handy in various
real-life situations.
The phrasebook will help
you ask for directions, clarify
a price, buy tickets, and
order food at a restaurant

T&P Books Publishing

PHRASEBOOK
CONTENTS

T&P Books Publishing

The bare minimum

Excuse me, ...	**Nu vă supărați, ...** [nu və supə'raʦ, ...]
Hello.	**Buna ziua.** [buna 'ziwa]
Thank you.	**Mulțumesc.** [mulʦu'mesk]
Good bye.	**La revedere.** [la reve'dere]
Yes.	**Da.** [da]
No.	**Nu.** [nu]
I don't know.	**Nu știu.** [nu 'ʃtiu]
Where? | Where to? | When?	**Unde? | Încotro? | Când?** [unde? | inko'tro? | kɨnd?]

I need ...	**Am nevoie de ...** [am ne'voje de ...]
I want ...	**Vreau ...** [vrʲau ...]
Do you have ...?	**Aveți ...?** [a'veʦ ...?]
Is there a ... here?	**Există ... aici?** [e'gzistə ... a'itʃi?]
May I ...?	**Pot ...?** [pot ...?]
..., please (polite request)	**..., vă rog** [..., və rog]

I'm looking for ...	**Caut ...** [kaut ...]
the restroom	**o toaletă** [o toa'letə]
an ATM	**un bancomat** [un banko'mat]
a pharmacy (drugstore)	**o farmacie** [o farma'ʧie]
a hospital	**un spital** [un spi'tal]
the police station	**o secție de poliție** [o 'sekʦie de po'liʦie]
the subway	**un metrou** [un me'trou]

a taxi	**un taxi** [un ta'ksi]
the train station	**o gară** [o 'garə]
My name is …	**Numele meu este …** [numele 'meu 'este …]
What's your name?	**Cum vă numiți?** [kum və nu'mitsʲ?]
Could you please help me?	**Mă puteți ajuta, vă rog?** [mə pu'tetsʲ aʒu'ta, və rog?]
I've got a problem.	**Am o problemă.** [am o pro'blemə]
I don't feel well.	**Mi-e rău.** [mi-e 'rəu]
Call an ambulance!	**Chemați o ambulanță!** [ke'matsʲ o ambu'lantsəl]
May I make a call?	**Pot să dau un telefon?** [pot sə dau un tele'fon?]
I'm sorry.	**Îmi pare rău.** [ɨmʲ 'pare rəu]
You're welcome.	**Cu plăcere.** [ku plə'tʃere]
I, me	**Eu** [eu]
you (inform.)	**tu** [tu]
he	**el** [el]
she	**ea** [ja]
they (masc.)	**ei** [ej]
they (fem.)	**ele** ['ele]
we	**noi** [noj]
you (pl)	**voi** [voj]
you (sg, form.)	**dumneavoastră** [dumnʲavo'astrə]
ENTRANCE	**INTRARE** [in'trare]
EXIT	**IEŞIRE** [je'ʃire]
OUT OF ORDER	**DEFECT** [de'fekt]
CLOSED	**ÎNCHIS** [ɨn'kis]

OPEN	**DESCHIS** [des'kis]
FOR WOMEN	**PENTRU FEMEI** [pentru fe'mej]
FOR MEN	**PENTRU BĂRBAȚI** [pentru bər'batsʲ]

Questions

Where?	**Unde?**
	['unde?]
Where to?	**Încotro?**
	[ɨnko'tro?]
Where from?	**De unde?**
	[de 'unde?]
Why?	**De ce?**
	[de ʧe?]
For what reason?	**Din ce motiv?**
	[din ʧe mo'tiv?]
When?	**Când?**
	[kɨnd?]

How long?	**Cât?**
	[kɨt?]
At what time?	**La ce oră?**
	[la ʧe 'ore?]
How much?	**Cât de mult?**
	[kɨt de mult?]
Do you have ...?	**Aveți ...?**
	[a'vetsʲ ...?]
Where is ...?	**Unde este ...?**
	[unde 'este ...?]

What time is it?	**Cât este ceasul?**
	[kɨt 'este 'ʧasul?]
May I make a call?	**Pot să dau un telefon?**
	[pot sə dau un tele'fon?]
Who's there?	**Cine e?**
	[ʧine e?]
Can I smoke here?	**Pot fuma aici?**
	[pot fu'ma a'iʧí?]
May I ...?	**Pot ...?**
	[pot ...?]

Needs

I'd like ...	**Aş dori ...** [aʃ do'ri ...]
I don't want ...	**Nu vreau ...** [nu 'vrʲau ...]
I'm thirsty.	**Mi-e sete.** [mi-e 'sete]
I want to sleep.	**Vreau să dorm.** [vrʲau sə dorm]

I want ...	**Vreau ...** [vrʲau ...]
to wash up	**să mă spăl** [sə mə spəl]
to brush my teeth	**să mă spăl pe dinţi** [sə mə spəl pe 'dinʦi]
to rest a while	**să mă odihnesc puţin** [sə mə odih'nesk pu'ʦin]
to change my clothes	**să mă schimb** [sə mə skimb]

to go back to the hotel	**să mă întorc la hotel** [sə mə ɨn'tork la ho'tel]
to buy ...	**să cumpăr ...** [sə 'kumpər ...]
to go to ...	**să merg la ...** [sə merg la ...]
to visit ...	**să vizitez ...** [sə vizi'tez ...]
to meet with ...	**să mă întâlnesc cu ...** [sə mə ɨntɨl'nesk ku ...]
to make a call	**să dau un telefon** [sə dau un tele'fon]

I'm tired.	**Sunt obosit /obosită/.** [sunt obo'sit /obo'sitə/]
We are tired.	**Suntem obosiţi.** [suntem obo'siʦi]
I'm cold.	**Mi-e frig.** [mi-e frig]
I'm hot.	**Mi-e cald.** [mi-e kald]
I'm OK.	**Sunt bine.** [sunt 'bine]

I need to make a call.

Trebuie să dau un telefon.
[trebuje sə dau un tele'fon]

I need to go to the restroom.

Trebuie să merg la toaletă.
[trebuje sə merg la toa'letə]

I have to go.

Chiar trebuie să plec.
[kjar 'trebuje sə plek]

I have to go now.

Trebuie să plec.
[trebuje sə plek]

Asking for directions

Excuse me, ...

Nu vă supărați, ...
[nu və supə'raʦ^j, ...]

Where is ...?

Unde este ...?
[unde 'este ...?]

Which way is ...?

În ce direcție este ...?
[ɨn ʧe di'rekʦie 'este ...?]

Could you help me, please?

Ați putea să mă ajutați, vă rog?
[aʦ^j put^ja sə mə aʒu'taʦ^j, və rog?]

I'm looking for ...

Caut ...
[kaut ...]

I'm looking for the exit.

Caut ieșirea.
[kaut 'eʃir^ja]

I'm going to ...

Urmează să ...
[ur'm^jazə sə ...]

Am I going the right way to ...?

Merg în direcția bună către ...?
[merg ɨn di'rekʦja 'bunə 'kɛtre ...?]

Is it far?

Este departe?
[este de'parte?]

Can I get there on foot?

Pot ajunge acolo pe jos?
[pot a'ʒunʒe a'kolo pe ʒos?]

Can you show me on the map?

Îmi puteți arăta pe hartă?
[ɨm^j pu'teʦ^j arə'ta pe 'hartə?]

Show me where we are right now.

Arătați-mi unde ne aflăm acum.
[arə'taʦi-mi 'unde ne afləm a'kum]

Here

Aici
[a'iʧi]

There

Acolo
[a'kolo]

This way

Pe aici
[pe a'iʧi]

Turn right.

Faceți dreapta.
[fa'ʧeʦ^j 'dr^japta]

Turn left.

Faceți stânga.
[fa'ʧeʦ^j 'stɨnga]

first (second, third) turn

prima (a doua, a treia)
[prima (a 'dowa, a 'treja)]

to the right

la dreapta
[la 'dr^japta]

to the left	**la stânga** [la 'stɨnga]
Go straight ahead.	**Mergeţi drept înainte.** [merdʒetsʲ drept ɨna'inte]

Signs

WELCOME!	**BINE AȚI VENIT!** [bine 'aṭsʲ ve'nit!]
ENTRANCE	**INTRARE** [in'trare]
EXIT	**IEȘIRE** [je'ʃire]

PUSH	**ÎMPINGEȚI** [im'pinʒeṭsʲ]
PULL	**TRAGEȚI** [tra'dʒeṭsʲ]
OPEN	**DESCHIS** [des'kis]
CLOSED	**ÎNCHIS** [in'kis]

FOR WOMEN	**PENTRU FEMEI** [pentru fe'mej]
FOR MEN	**PENTRU BĂRBAȚI** [pentru bər'baṭsʲ]
GENTLEMEN, GENTS	**BĂRBAȚI** [bər'baṭsʲ]
WOMEN	**FEMEI** [fe'mej]

DISCOUNTS	**REDUCERI** [re'dutʃerʲ]
SALE	**OFERTĂ** [o'fertə]
FREE	**GRATUIT** [gratu'it]
NEW!	**NOU!** ['nou!]
ATTENTION!	**ATENȚIE!** [a'tenṭsie!]

NO VACANCIES	**NU MAI SUNT CAMERE DISPONIBILE** [nu maj sunt 'kamere dispo'nibile]
RESERVED	**REZERVAT** [rezer'vat]
ADMINISTRATION	**CONDUCERE** [kon'dutʃere]
STAFF ONLY	**REZERVAT PERSONAL** [rezer'vat perso'nal]

BEWARE OF THE DOG!

NO SMOKING!

DO NOT TOUCH!

DANGEROUS

DANGER

HIGH VOLTAGE

NO SWIMMING!

ATENȚIE, CÂINE RĂU!
[a'tentsie, 'kijne rəu!]

FUMATUL INTERZIS!
[fu'matul inter'zis!]

A NU SE ATINGE!
[a nu se a'tinʒe!]

PERICOL
[pe'rikol]

PERICOL GENERAL
[pe'rikol dʒene'ral]

ATENȚIE ÎNALTĂ TENSIUNE
[a'tentsie ɨnaltə tensi'une]

ÎNOTUL INTERZIS!
[ɨ'notul inter'zis!]

OUT OF ORDER

FLAMMABLE

FORBIDDEN

NO TRESPASSING!

WET PAINT

DEFECT
[de'fekt]

INFLAMABIL
[infla'mabil]

INTERZIS
[inter'zis]

ACCES INTERZIS!
[aktʃes inter'zis!]

PROASPĂT VOPSIT
[pro'aspət vop'sit]

CLOSED FOR RENOVATIONS

WORKS AHEAD

DETOUR

ÎNCHIS PENTRU RENOVARE
[ɨn'kis 'pentru reno'vare]

ATENȚIE SE LUCREAZĂ
[a'tentsie se lu'krʲazə]

TRAFIC DEVIAT
[trafik de'vjat]

Transportation. General phrases

plane	**avion** [a'vjon]
train	**tren** [tren]
bus	**autobuz** [auto'buz]
ferry	**feribot** [feri'bot]
taxi	**taxi** [ta'ksi]
car	**maşină** [ma'ʃinə]

schedule	**orar** [o'rar]
Where can I see the schedule?	**Unde pot vedea orarul?** [unde pot ve'dʲa o'rarul?]
workdays (weekdays)	**zile de lucru** [zile de 'lukru]
weekends	**sfârşit de săptămână** [sfir'ʃit de septe'minə]
holidays	**sărbători** [serbeto'ri]

DEPARTURE	**PLECĂRI** [plekərʲ]
ARRIVAL	**SOSIRI** [so'sirʲ]
DELAYED	**ÎNTÂRZIERI** [intirzi'erʲ]
CANCELLED	**ANULĂRI** [anulərʲ]

next (train, etc.)	**următorul** [urme'torul]
first	**primul** ['primul]
last	**ultimul** ['ultimul]

When is the next ...?	**Când este următorul ...?** [kind 'este urme'torul ...?]
When is the first ...?	**Când este primul ...?** [kind 'este 'primul ...?]

When is the last ...?

Când este ultimul ...?
[kɨnd 'este 'ultimul ...?]

transfer (change of trains, etc.)

schimb
[skimb]

to make a transfer

a schimba
[a skim'ba]

Do I need to make a transfer?

**Trebuie să schimb ...
(trenul | avionul)?**
[trebuje sə skimb ...
('trenul | a'vjonul)?]

Buying tickets

Where can I buy tickets?	**De unde pot cumpăra bilete?** [de 'unde pot kumpǝ'ra bi'lete?]
ticket	**bilet** [bi'let]
to buy a ticket	**a cumpăra un bilet** [a kumpǝ'ra un bi'let]
ticket price	**prețul biletului** [pretsul bi'letului]
Where to?	**În ce direcție?** [ɨn tʃe di'rektsie?]
To what station?	**La ce stație?** [la tʃe 'statsie?]
I need …	**Am nevoie de …** [am ne'voje de …]
one ticket	**un bilet** [un bi'let]
two tickets	**două bilete** [dowǝ bi'lete]
three tickets	**trei bilete** [trej bi'lete]
one-way	**dus** [dus]
round-trip	**dus-întors** [dus-ɨn'tors]
first class	**clasa întâi** [klasa ɨn'tɨj]
second class	**clasa a doua** [klasa a 'dowa]
today	**astăzi** [astǝzʲ]
tomorrow	**mâine** [mɨjne]
the day after tomorrow	**poimâine** [po'imɨine]
in the morning	**dimineața** [dimi'nʲatsa]
in the afternoon	**după-masa** ['dupǝ-'masa]
in the evening	**seara** [sʲara]

aisle seat	**loc la culoar** [lok la kulo'ar]
window seat	**loc la geam** [lok la ʤʲam]
How much?	**Cât costă?** [kɨt 'kostə?]
Can I pay by credit card?	**Pot plăti cu cardul?** [pot plə'ti ku 'kardul?]

Bus

bus	**autobuz** [auto'buz]
intercity bus	**autobuz interurban** [auto'buz interur'ban]
bus stop	**stație de autobuz** [statsie de auto'buz]
Where's the nearest bus stop?	**Unde este cea mai apropiată stație de autobuz?** [unde 'este tʃa maj apro'pjatə 'statsie de auto'buz?]

number (bus ~, etc.)	**număr** ['numər]
Which bus do I take to get to ...?	**Ce autobuz trebuie să iau să ajung la ...?** [tʃe auto'buz tre'buje sə jau sə a'ʒun la ...?]
Does this bus go to ...?	**Acest autobuz ajunge la ...?** [a'tʃest auto'buz a'ʒunʒe la ...?]
How frequent are the buses?	**La ce interval vin autobuzele?** [la tʃe inter'val vin auto'buzele?]

every 15 minutes	**la fiecare 15 minute** [la fie'kare 'tʃintʃsprezetʃe mi'nute]
every half hour	**la fiecare jumătate de oră** [la fie'kare ʒumə'tate de 'orə]
every hour	**la fiecare oră** [la fie'kare 'orə]
several times a day	**de câteva ori pe zi** [de kite'va ori pe zi]
... times a day	**de ... ori pe zi** [de ... ori pe zi]

schedule	**orar** [o'rar]
Where can I see the schedule?	**Unde pot vedea orarul?** [unde pot ve'dʲa o'rarul?]
When is the next bus?	**Când este următorul autobuz?** [kind 'este urmə'torul auto'buz?]
When is the first bus?	**Când este primul autobuz?** [kind 'este 'primul auto'buz?]
When is the last bus?	**Când este ultimul autobuz?** [kind 'este 'ultimul auto'buz?]

stop	**stație** [statsie]
next stop	**următoarea stație** [urmeto'ar'a 'statsie]
last stop (terminus)	**ultima stație** [ultima 'statsie]
Stop here, please.	**Opriți aici, vă rog.** [o'prits' a'itʃi, və rog]
Excuse me, this is my stop.	**Scuzați-mă, cobor aici.** [sku'zatsi-mə, ko'bor a'itʃi]

Train

train	**tren** [tren]
suburban train	**tren suburban** [tren subur'ban]
long-distance train	**tren pe distanță lungă** [tren pe dis'tantse 'lunge]
train station	**o gară** [o 'gare]
Excuse me, where is the exit to the platform?	**Scuzați-mă, unde este ieșirea** **spre peron?** [sku'zatsi-me, 'unde 'este ie'ʃirʲa spre pe'ron?]

Does this train go to …?	**Acest tren merge la …?** [a'tʃest tren 'merdʒe la …?]
next train	**următorul tren** [urme'torul tren]
When is the next train?	**Când este următorul tren?** [kind 'este urme'torul tren?]
Where can I see the schedule?	**Unde pot vedea mersul trenurilor?** [unde pot ve'dʲa 'mersul 'trenurilor?]
From which platform?	**De la care peron?** [de la kare pe'ron?]
When does the train arrive in …?	**Când ajunge trenul la …?** [kind a'ʒundʒe 'trenul la …?]

Please help me.	**Vă rog să mă ajutați.** [ve rog se me aʒu'tatsi]
I'm looking for my seat.	**Îmi caut locul.** [imʲ 'kaut 'lokul]
We're looking for our seats.	**Ne căutăm locurile.** [ne keutem 'lokurile]

My seat is taken.	**Locul meu este ocupat.** [lokul 'meu 'este oku'pat]
Our seats are taken.	**Locurile noastre sunt ocupate.** [lokurile no'astre sunt oku'pate]
I'm sorry but this is my seat.	**Îmi pare rău dar acesta** **este locul meu.** [imʲ 'pare reu dar a'tʃesta 'este 'lokul 'meu]

Is this seat taken?

Este liber acest loc?
[este 'liber a'tʃest lok?]

May I sit here?

Pot să stau aici?
[pot se 'stau a'itʃi?]

On the train. Dialogue (No ticket)

Ticket, please.

Biletul la control.
[bi'letul la kon'trol]

I don't have a ticket.

Nu am bilet.
[nu am bi'let]

I lost my ticket.

Mi-am pierdut biletul.
[mi-am 'pjerdut bi'letul]

I forgot my ticket at home.

Mi-am uitat biletul acasă.
[mi-am 'ujtat bi'letul a'kasə]

You can buy a ticket from me.

Puteţi cumpăra un bilet de la mine.
[pu'tetsʲ kumpə'ra un bi'let de la 'mine]

You will also have to pay a fine.

**Va trebui, de asemenea,
să plătiţi şi o amendă.**
[va 'trebuj, de a'semenʲa,
sə plə'titsʲ ʃi o a'mendə]

Okay.

Bine.
['bine]

Where are you going?

Unde mergeţi?
[unde mer'dʒetsi?]

I'm going to …

Merg la …
[merg la …]

How much? I don't understand.

Cât costă? Nu înţeleg.
[kɨt 'kostə? nu ɨntse'leg]

Write it down, please.

Scrieţi pe ceva, vă rog.
[skri'etsʲ pe tʃe'va, və rog]

Okay. Can I pay with a credit card?

Bine. Pot plăti cu cardul?
[bine. pot plə'ti ku 'kardul?]

Yes, you can.

Da, puteţi.
[da, pu'tetsʲ]

Here's your receipt.

Aceasta este chitanţa dumneavoastră.
[a'tʃasta 'este ki'tantsa dumnʲavo'astrə]

Sorry about the fine.

Îmi pare rău pentru amendă.
[ɨmʲ 'pare rəu 'pentru a'mendə]

That's okay. It was my fault.

Este în regulă. A fost vina mea.
[este ɨn 'regulə. a fost 'vina mʲa]

Enjoy your trip.

Călătorie plăcută!
[kələto'rie plə'kutə!]

Taxi

taxi
taxi
[ta'ksi]

taxi driver
șofer de taxi
[ʃo'fer de ta'ksi]

to catch a taxi
a lua un taxi
[a 'lua un ta'ksi]

taxi stand
stație de taxiuri
[staʦie de ta'ksjurʲ]

Where can I get a taxi?
De unde pot lua un taxi?
[de 'unde pot 'lua un ta'ksi?]

to call a taxi
a chema un taxi
[a 'kema un ta'ksi]

I need a taxi.
Am nevoie de un taxi.
[am ne'voje de un ta'ksi]

Right now.
Acum.
[a'kum]

What is your address (location)?
Care este adresa dumneavoastră?
[kare 'este a'dresa dumnʲavo'astrə?]

My address is …
Adresa mea este …
[a'dresa mʲa 'este …]

Your destination?
Unde mergeți?
[unde mer'dʒeʦi?]

Excuse me, …
Scuzați-mă, …
[sku'zaʦi-mə, …]

Are you available?
Sunteți liber?
[sun'teʦʲ 'liber?]

How much is it to get to …?
Cât costă până la …?
[kɨt 'kostə 'pɨnə la …?]

Do you know where it is?
Știți unde este?
[ʃtiʦʲ 'unde 'este?]

Airport, please.
La aeroport, vă rog.
[la aero'port, və rog]

Stop here, please.
Opriți aici, vă rog.
[o'priʦʲ a'itʃi, və rog]

It's not here.
Nu este aici.
[nu 'este a'itʃi]

This is the wrong address.
Adresa asta este greșită.
[a'dresa as'ta 'este gre'ʃitə]

Turn left.
Luați-o la stânga.
[lu'aʦi-o la 'stɨnga]

Turn right.
Luați-o la dreapta.
[lu'aʦi-o la 'drʲapta]

How much do I owe you?	**Cât vă datorez?**
	[kɨt və da'torez?]
I'd like a receipt, please.	**Aş dori o chitanţă, vă rog.**
	[aʃ do'ri o ki'tantsə, və rog]
Keep the change.	**Păstraţi restul.**
	[pəs'tratsʲ 'restul]

Would you please wait for me?	**Mă puteţi aştepta, vă rog?**
	[mə pu'tetsʲ aʃtep'ta, və rog?]
five minutes	**cinci minute**
	[tʃintʃ mi'nute]
ten minutes	**zece minute**
	[zetʃe mi'nute]
fifteen minutes	**cincisprezece minute**
	[tʃintʃisprezetʃe mi'nute]
twenty minutes	**douăzeci de minute**
	[dowə'zetʃi de mi'nute]
half an hour	**o jumătate de oră**
	[o ʒumə'tate de 'orə]

Hotel

Hello.	**Bună ziua.** [bunə 'ziwa]
My name is …	**Mă numesc …** [mə nu'mesk …]
I have a reservation.	**Am o rezervare.** [am o rezer'vare]
I need …	**Am nevoie de …** [am ne'voje de …]
a single room	**o cameră single** [o 'kamerə 'singlə]
a double room	**o cameră dublă** [o 'kamerə 'dublə]
How much is that?	**Cât costă?** [kɨt 'kostə?]
That's a bit expensive.	**Este puțin cam scump.** [este pu'ʦin kam skump]
Do you have anything else?	**Mai există alte opțiuni?** [maj e'gzistə 'alte op'ʦjuni?]
I'll take it.	**O iau.** [o 'jau]
I'll pay in cash.	**Plătesc în numerar.** [plə'tesk ɨn nume'rar]
I've got a problem.	**Am o problemă.** [am o pro'blemə]
My … is broken.	**… este stricat /stricată/.** [… 'este stri'kat /stri'katə/]
My … is out of order.	**… este defect /defectă/.** [… 'este de'fekt /'este de'fektə/]
TV	**Meu televizorul (este stricat)** [meu televi'zorul ('este stri'kat)]
air conditioner	**Aerul meu condiționat (este defect)** [aerul 'meu kondiʦjo'nat ('este de'fekt)]
tap	**Meu robinetul (este stricat)** [meu robi'netul ('este stri'kat)]
shower	**Meu dușul (este stricat)** [meu 'duʃul ('este stri'kat)]
sink	**Mea chiuveta (este defectă)** [mʲa kju'veta ('este de'fektə)]
safe	**Meu seiful (este stricat)** [meu 'sejful ('este stri'kat)]

door lock	Încuietoarea (este defectă)
	[ɪnkue'toarʲa]
electrical outlet	Mea priza (este defectă)
	[mʲa 'priza ('este de'fektə)]
hairdryer	Uscătorul meu de păr (este stricat)
	[uskə'torul 'meu de pər ('este stri'kat)]

I don't have ...	Nu am ...
	[nu am ...]
water	apă
	['apə]
light	lumină
	[lu'minə]
electricity	curent electric
	[ku'rent e'lektric]

Can you give me ...?	Îmi puteți da ...?
	[ɪmʲ pu'tetsʲ da ...?]
a towel	un prosop
	[un pro'sop]
a blanket	o pătură
	[o 'pəturə]
slippers	papuci
	[pa'putʃi]
a robe	un halat
	[un ha'lat]
shampoo	nişte şampon
	[ʃam'pon]
soap	nişte săpun
	[sə'pun]

I'd like to change rooms.	Aş dori să îmi schimb camera.
	[aʃ do'ri sə ɪmj skimb 'kamera]
I can't find my key.	Nu îmi găsesc cheia.
	[nu ɪmj gə'sesk ke'ja]
Could you open my room, please?	Puteți să îmi deschideți camera, vă rog?
	[pu'tetsʲ sə ɪmʲ de'skidetsʲ 'kamera, ve rog?]
Who's there?	Cine e?
	[tʃine e?]
Come in!	Intraţi!
	[in'tratsʲ!]
Just a minute!	Un minut!
	[un mi'nut!]

Not right now, please.	Nu acum, vă rog.
	[nu a'kum, ve rog]
Come to my room, please.	Veniţi în camera mea, vă rog.
	[ve'nitsʲ ɪn 'kamera mʲa, ve rog]

I'd like to order food service.

Aş dori să îmi comand de mâncare în cameră.
[aʃ do'ri sə imj ko'mand de min'kare in 'kamerə]

My room number is ...

Numărul camerei mele este ...
[numərul 'kamerej mele 'este ...]

I'm leaving ...

Plec ...
[plek ...]

We're leaving ...

Plecăm ...
[plekəm ...]

right now

acum
[a'kum]

this afternoon

în această după-masă
[in a'tʃastə 'dupə-'masə]

tonight

diseară
[di'sʲarə]

tomorrow

mâine
[mijne]

tomorrow morning

mâine dimineaţă
[mijne dimi'nʲatsə]

tomorrow evening

mâine seară
[mijne 'sʲarə]

the day after tomorrow

poimâine
[po'imiine]

I'd like to pay.

Aş dori să plătesc.
[aʃ do'ri sə plə'tesk]

Everything was wonderful.

Totul a fost excelent.
[totul a fost ekstʃe'lent]

Where can I get a taxi?

De unde pot lua un taxi?
[de 'unde pot 'lua un ta'ksi?]

Would you call a taxi for me, please?

Îmi puteţi chema un taxi, vă rog?
[imʲ pu'tetsʲ ke'ma un ta'ksi, və rog?]

Restaurant

Can I look at the menu, please?
Pot vedea meniul, vă rog?
[pot ve'dʲa me'njul, və rog?]

Table for one.
O masă pentru o persoană.
[o 'masə 'pentru o perso'anə]

There are two (three, four) of us.
Suntem două (trei, patru) persoane.
[suntem 'dowə (trej, 'patru) perso'ane]

Smoking
Fumători
[fumə'tori]

No smoking
Nefumători
[nefumə'tori]

Excuse me! (addressing a waiter)
Scuzați-mă!
[sku'zatsi-mə!]

menu
meniu
[me'nju]

wine list
lista de vinuri
[lista de 'vinuri]

The menu, please.
Un meniu, vă rog.
[un me'nju, və rog]

Are you ready to order?
Sunteți gata să comandați?
[sun'tetsʲ 'gata sə koman'datsʲ?]

What will you have?
Ce veți servi?
[tʃe 'vetsi ser'vi?]

I'll have …
Vreau …
[vrʲau …]

I'm a vegetarian.
Sunt vegetarian.
[sunt vedʒeta'rjan /vedʒeta'rjanə/]

meat
carne
['karne]

fish
peşte
['peʃte]

vegetables
legume
[le'gume]

Do you have vegetarian dishes?
Aveți feluri de mâncare vegetariene?
[a'vetsʲ fe'luri de mɨn'kare vedʒe'tariene?]

I don't eat pork.
Nu mănânc porc.
[nu mə'nɨnk pork]

Band-Aid
El /Ea/ nu mănâncă carne.
[el /ʲa/ nu mə'nɨnkə 'karne]

I am allergic to …
Sunt alergic la …
[sunt a'lerdʒik /a'lerdʒikə/ la …]

Would you please bring me ...

Vă rog frumos, îmi puteți aduce ...
[və rog fru'mos, ɨmj pu'tetsʲ a'dutʃe ...]

salt | pepper | sugar

sare | piper | zahăr
[sare | pi'per | 'zahər]

coffee | tea | dessert

cafea | ceai | desert
[ka'fʲa | tʃaj | de'sert]

water | sparkling | plain

apă | minerală | plată
[apə | mine'ralə | 'platə]

a spoon | fork | knife

o lingură | o furculiță | un cuțit
[o 'lingurə | o furku'litsə | un ku'tsit]

a plate | napkin

o farfurie | un șervețel
[o farfu'rie | un ʃerve'tsel]

Enjoy your meal!

Poftă bună!
[poftə 'bunə!]

One more, please.

Încă unul /unula/, vă rog.
[ɨnkə 'unul /'unula/, və rog]

It was very delicious.

A fost foarte bun.
[a fost fo'arte bun]

check | change | tip

notă | rest | bacșiș
[notə | rest | bak'ʃiʃ]

Check, please.
(Could I have the check, please?)

Nota, vă rog.
[nota, və rog]

Can I pay by credit card?

Pot plăti cu cardul?
[pot plə'ti ku 'kardul?]

I'm sorry, there's a mistake here.

Îmi pare rău, este o greșeală aici.
[ɨmʲ 'pare rəu, 'este o gre'ʃalə a'itʃi]

Shopping

Can I help you?	**Pot să vă ajut?** [pot sə və a'ʒut?]
Do you have ...?	**Aveți ...?** [a'vetsʲ ...?]
I'm looking for ...	**Caut ...** [kaut ...]
I need ...	**Am nevoie de ...** [am ne'voje de ...]

I'm just looking.	**Doar mă uit.** [do'ar mə uit]
We're just looking.	**Doar ne uităm.** [do'ar ne uitəm]
I'll come back later.	**Mă întorc mai târziu.** [mə ɨn'tork maj tɨr'zju]
We'll come back later.	**Ne întoarcem mai târziu.** [ne ɨnto'artʃem maj tɨr'zju]
discounts | sale	**reduceri | ofertă** [re'dutʃerʲ | o'fertə]

Would you please show me ...	**Îmi puteți arăta ..., vă rog.** [ɨmʲ pu'tetsʲ arə'ta ..., və rog]
Would you please give me ...	**Îmi puteți da ..., vă rog.** [ɨmʲ pu'tetsʲ da ..., və rog]
Can I try it on?	**Pot să probez?** [pot sə pro'bez?]
Excuse me, where's the fitting room?	**Nu vă supărați, unde este cabina de probă?** [nu və supə'ratsʲ, 'unde 'este ka'bina de 'probə?]
Which color would you like?	**Ce culoare ați dori?** [tʃe kulo'are 'atsʲ do'ri?]
size | length	**mărime | lungime** [mə'rime | lun'dʒime]
How does it fit?	**Cum vine?** [kum 'vine?]

How much is it?	**Cât costă asta?** [kɨt 'kostə 'asta?]
That's too expensive.	**Este prea scump.** [este pr'a skump]
I'll take it.	**Îl iau /O iau/.** [ɨl 'jau /o 'jau/]

Excuse me, where do I pay?	**Nu vă supărați, unde plătesc?**
	[nu və supə'raʦʲ, 'unde plə'tesk?]
Will you pay in cash or credit card?	**Plătiți în numerar sau cu cardul?**
	[plə'tiʦʲ in nume'rar sau ku 'kardul?]
In cash | with credit card	**În numerar | cu cardul**
	[in nume'rar | ku 'kardul]

Do you want the receipt?	**Doriți chitanță?**
	[do'riʦʲ ki'tanʦə?]
Yes, please.	**Da, vă rog.**
	[da, və rog]
No, it's OK.	**Nu, este în regulă.**
	[nu, 'este in 'regulə]
Thank you. Have a nice day!	**Mulțumesc. O zi bună!**
	[mulʦu'mesk. o zi 'bunə!]

In town

Excuse me, ...
Îmi cer scuze.
[ɨmʲ tʃer 'skuze]

I'm looking for ...
Caut ...
[kaut ...]

the subway
metroul
[me'troul]

my hotel
hotelul
[ho'telul]

the movie theater
cinematograful
[tʃinemato'graful]

a taxi stand
o stație de taxi
[o 'statsie de ta'ksi]

an ATM
un bancomat
[un banko'mat]

a foreign exchange office
un birou de schimb valutar
[un bi'rou de skimb valu'tar]

an internet café
un internet café
[un inter'net kafé]

... street
... strada
[... 'strada]

this place
locul acesta
[lokul a'tʃesta]

Do you know where ... is?
Știți unde este ...?
[ʃtitsʲ 'unde 'este ...?]

Which street is this?
Ce stradă este aceasta?
[tʃe 'strade 'este a'tʃasta?]

Show me where we are right now.
Arătați-mi unde ne aflăm acum.
[are'tatsi-mi 'unde ne aflem a'kum]

Can I get there on foot?
Pot ajunge acolo pe jos?
[pot a'ʒunʒe a'kolo pe ʒos?]

Do you have a map of the city?
Aveți o hartă a orașului?
[a'vetsʲ o 'harte a ora'ʃului?]

How much is a ticket to get in?
Cât costă un bilet de intrare?
[kɨt 'koste un bi'let de in'trare?]

Can I take pictures here?
Este permis fotografiatul aici?
[este per'mis fotogra'fjatul a'itʃi?]

Are you open?
Este deschis?
[este des'kis?]

When do you open?

La ce oră deschideți?
[la tʃe 'orə des'kidetsʲ?]

When do you close?

La ce oră închideți?
[la tʃe 'orə in'kidetsʲ?]

Money

money	**bani** ['bani]
cash	**numerar** [nume'rar]
paper money	**bancnote** [bank'note]
loose change	**mărunțiș** [mərun'tsiʃ]
check | change | tip	**notă | rest | bacșiș** [notə | rest | bak'ʃiʃ]
credit card	**card bancar** [kard ban'kar]
wallet	**portofel** [porto'fel]
to buy	**a cumpăra** [a kumpə'ra]
to pay	**a plăti** [a plə'ti]
fine	**amendă** [a'mendə]
free	**gratis** [gratis]
Where can I buy ...?	**De unde pot cumpăra ...?** [de 'unde pot kumpə'ra ...?]
Is the bank open now?	**Banca este deschisă acum?** [banka 'este des'kisə a'kum?]
When does it open?	**Când deschide?** [kɨnd des'kide?]
When does it close?	**Când închide?** [kɨnd ɨn'kide?]
How much?	**Cât costă?** [kɨt 'kostə?]
How much is this?	**Cât costă asta?** [kɨt 'kostə 'asta?]
That's too expensive.	**Este prea scump.** [este prʲa skump]
Excuse me, where do I pay?	**Nu vă supărați, unde plătesc?** [nu və supə'ratsʲ, 'unde plə'tesk?]
Check, please.	**Nota, vă rog.** [nota, və rog]

Can I pay by credit card? | **Pot plăti cu cardul?**
[pot plə'ti ku 'kardul?]

Is there an ATM here? | **Există vreun bancomat aici?**
[e'gzistə 'vreun banko'mat a'itʃi?]

I'm looking for an ATM. | **Caut un bancomat.**
[kaut un banko'mat]

I'm looking for a foreign exchange office. | **Caut un birou de schimb valutar.**
[kaut un bi'rou de skimb valu'tar]

I'd like to change ... | **Aş dori să schimb ...**
[aʃ do'ri sə skimb ...]

What is the exchange rate? | **Care este cursul de schimb?**
[kare 'este 'kursul de skimb?]

Do you need my passport? | **Vă trebuie paşaportul meu?**
[və 'trebuje paʃa'portul 'meu?]

Time

What time is it?	**Cât este ceasul?** [kɨt 'este 'tʃasul?]
When?	**Când?** [kɨnd?]
At what time?	**La ce oră?** [la tʃe 'orə?]
now | later | after …	**acum | mai târziu | după …** [a'kum | maj tɨr'zju | 'dupə …]

one o'clock	**ora unu** [ora 'unu]
one fifteen	**unu şi un sfert** [unu ʃi un sfert]
one thirty	**unu şi jumătate** [unu ʃi ʒumə'tate]
one forty-five	**unu patruzeci şi cinci** [unu patru'zetʃ ʃi 'tʃintʃ]

one | two | three	**unu | două | trei** [unu | 'dowə | trej]
four | five | six	**patru | cinci | şase** [patru | 'tʃintʃ | 'ʃase]
seven | eight | nine	**şapte | opt | nouă** [ʃapte | opt | 'nowə]
ten | eleven | twelve	**zece | unsprezece | doisprezece** [zetʃe | 'unsprezetʃe | 'dojsprezetʃe]

in …	**în …** [ɨn …]
five minutes	**cinci minute** [tʃintʃ mi'nute]
ten minutes	**zece minute** [zetʃe mi'nute]
fifteen minutes	**cincisprezece minute** [tʃintʃisprezetʃe mi'nute]
twenty minutes	**douăzeci de minute** [dowə'zetʃi de mi'nute]
half an hour	**într-o jumătate de oră** [ɨntr-o ʒumə'tate de 'orə]
an hour	**într-o oră** [ɨntr-o 'orə]

in the morning	**dimineața** [dimi'nʲatsa]
early in the morning	**dimineața devreme** [dimi'nʲatsa de'vreme]
this morning	**dimineața aceasta** [dimi'nʲatsa a'tʃasta]
tomorrow morning	**mâine dimineață** [mɨjne dimi'nʲatsə]
in the middle of the day	**la prânz** [la prɨnz]
in the afternoon	**după-masa** ['dupə-'masa]
in the evening	**seara** [sʲara]
tonight	**diseară** [di'sʲarə]
at night	**noaptea** [no'aptʲa]
yesterday	**ieri** [jerʲ]
today	**azi** [azʲ]
tomorrow	**mâine** [mɨjne]
the day after tomorrow	**poimâine** [po'imɨine]
What day is it today?	**Ce zi este astăzi?** [tʃe zi 'este astəzʲ?]
It's ...	**Azi este ...** [azʲ 'este ...]
Monday	**Luni** [lunʲ]
Tuesday	**Marți** [martsʲ]
Wednesday	**Miercuri** [mjerkurʲ]
Thursday	**Joi** [ʒoj]
Friday	**Vineri** [vinerʲ]
Saturday	**Sâmbătă** [sɨmbətə]
Sunday	**Duminică** [du'minikə]

Greetings. Introductions

Hello.	**Bună ziua.** [bunə 'ziwa]
Pleased to meet you.	**Îmi pare bine.** [im^j 'pare 'bine]
Me too.	**Şi mie.** [ʃi 'mie]
I'd like you to meet ...	**Aş vrea să vă fac cunoştinţă cu ...** [aʃ 'vrʲa sə və fak kunoʃ'tintsə ku ...]
Nice to meet you.	**Mă bucur de cunoştinţă.** [mə bukur de kunoʃ'tintsə]
How are you?	**Ce mai faceţi?** [tʃe maj 'fatʃetsʲ?]
My name is ...	**Mă numesc ...** [mə nu'mesk ...]
His name is ...	**El este ...** [el 'este ...]
Her name is ...	**Ea este ...** [ʲa 'este ...]
What's your name?	**Cum vă numiţi?** [kum və nu'mitsʲ?]
What's his name?	**Cum se numeşte dumnealui?** [kum se nu'meʃte dum'nalui?]
What's her name?	**Cum se numeşte dumneaei?** [kum se nu'meʃte dumna'ej?]
What's your last name?	**Care este numele dumneavoastră de familie?** [kare 'este 'numele dumnʲavo'astrə de fa'milie?]
You can call me ...	**Îmi puteţi spune ...** [im^j pu'tetsʲ 'spune ...]
Where are you from?	**De unde sunteţi?** [de 'unde 'suntetsʲ?]
I'm from ...	**Sunt din ...** [sunt din ...]
What do you do for a living?	**Cu ce vă ocupaţi?** [ku tʃe və oku'patsʲ?]
Who is this?	**Cine este acesta /aceasta/?** [tʃine 'este a'tʃesta /a'tʃasta/?]
Who is he?	**Cine este el?** [tʃine 'este el?]

Who is she?	**Cine este ea?** [tʃine 'este ja?]
Who are they?	**Cine sunt ei /ele/?** [tʃine sunt ej /'ele/?]

This is ...	**Acesta /Aceasta/ este ...** [a'tʃesta /a'tʃasta/ 'este ...]
my friend (masc.)	**prietenul meu** [pri'etenul 'meu]
my friend (fem.)	**prietena mea** [pri'etena mʲa]
my husband	**soțul meu** [soʦul 'meu]
my wife	**soția mea** [so'ʦia mʲa]

my father	**tatăl meu** [tatəl 'meu]
my mother	**mama mea** [mama mʲa]
my brother	**fratele meu** [fratele 'meu]
my sister	**sora mea** [sora mʲa]
my son	**fiul meu** [fjul 'meu]
my daughter	**fiica mea** [fiika mʲa]

This is our son.	**Acesta este fiul nostru.** [a'tʃesta 'este fjul 'nostru]
This is our daughter.	**Aceasta este fiica noastră.** [a'tʃasta 'este 'fiika no'astrə]
These are my children.	**Aceştia sunt copiii mei.** [a'tʃeʃtja sunt ko'piij mej]
These are our children.	**Aceştia sunt copiii noştri.** [a'tʃeʃtja sunt ko'piij 'noʃtri]

Farewells

Good bye! **Le revedere!**
[le reve'dere!]

Bye! (inform.) **Pa!**
[pa!]

See you tomorrow. **Pe mâine.**
[pe 'mɨine]

See you soon. **Pe curând.**
[pe ku'rɨnd]

See you at seven. **Ne vedem la şapte.**
[ne ve'dem la 'ʃapte]

Have fun! **Distracţie plăcută!**
[dis'traktsie plə'kutə!]

Talk to you later. **Ne auzim mai târziu.**
[ne au'zim maj tɨr'zju]

Have a nice weekend. **Week-end plăcut.**
[wi'kend plə'kut]

Good night. **Noapte bună.**
[no'apte 'bunə]

It's time for me to go. **E timpul să mă retrag.**
[e 'timpul sə mə re'trag]

I have to go. **Trebuie să plec.**
[trebuje sə plek]

I will be right back. **Revin imediat.**
[re'vin ime'djat]

It's late. **Este târziu.**
[este tɨr'zju]

I have to get up early. **Trebuie să mă trezesc devreme.**
[trebuje sə mə tre'zesk de'vreme]

I'm leaving tomorrow. **Plec mâine.**
[plek 'mɨine]

We're leaving tomorrow. **Plecăm mâine.**
[plekəm 'mɨine]

Have a nice trip! **Călătorie plăcută!**
[kələto'rie plə'kutə!]

It was nice meeting you. **Mi-a părut bine de cunoştinţă.**
[mia pə'rut 'bine de kunoʃ'tintsə]

It was nice talking to you. **Mi-a părut bine să stăm de vorbă.**
[mia pə'rut 'bine sə stəm de 'vorbə]

Thanks for everything. **Vă mulţumesc pentru tot.**
[və mulʃsu'mesk 'pentru tot]

I had a very good time.

M-am simțit foarte bine.
[mam sim'tsit fo'arte 'bine]

We had a very good time.

Ne-am simțit foarte bine.
[ne-am sim'tsit fo'arte 'bine]

It was really great.

A fost minunat.
[a fost minu'nat]

I'm going to miss you.

O să îți simt lipsa.
[o sə 'itsʲ simt 'lipsa]

We're going to miss you.

Îți vom simți lipsa.
[itsʲ vom 'simtsʲ 'lipsa]

Good luck!

Noroc!
[no'rok!]

Say hi to …

Salută-l pe… /Salut-o pe …/
[sa'lutəl pe… /sa'luto pe …/]

Foreign language

I don't understand.	**Nu înțeleg.** [nu inʦe'leg]
Write it down, please.	**Scrieți pe ceva, vă rog.** [skri'eʦ' pe ʧe'va, və rog]
Do you speak ...?	**Vorbiți ...?** [vor'biʦ' ...?]

I speak a little bit of ...	**Vorbesc puțină ...** [vor'besk pu'ʦinə ...]
English	**engleză** [en'glezə]
Turkish	**turcă** ['turkə]
Arabic	**arabă** [a'rabə]
French	**franceză** [fran'ʧezə]

German	**germană** [ʤer'manə]
Italian	**italiană** [itali'anə]
Spanish	**spaniolă** [spa'njolə]
Portuguese	**portugheză** [portu'gezə]
Chinese	**chineză** [ki'nezə]
Japanese	**japoneză** [ʒapo'nezə]

Can you repeat that, please.	**Vă rog să repetați.** [və rog sə repe'taʦ']
I understand.	**Am înțeles.** [am inʦe'les]
I don't understand.	**Nu înțeleg.** [nu inʦe'leg]
Please speak more slowly.	**Vă rog să vorbiți mai rar.** [və rog sə vor'biʦ' maj rar]

Is that correct? (Am I saying it right?)	**Aşa se spune?** [a'ʃa se 'spune?]
What is this? (What does this mean?)	**Ce e asta?** [ʧe e 'asta?]

Apologies

Excuse me, please.	**Îmi cer scuze.** [im^j ʧer 'skuze]
I'm sorry.	**Îmi pare rău.** [im^j 'pare rəu]
I'm really sorry.	**Îmi pare foarte rău.** [im^j 'pare fo'arte rəu]
Sorry, it's my fault.	**Scuze, este vina mea.** [skuze, 'este 'vina m^ja]
My mistake.	**Am greşit.** [am gre'ʃit]
May I ...?	**Aş putea ...?** [aʃ pu't^ja ...?]
Do you mind if I ...?	**Vă deranjează dacă ...?** [və deran'ʒ^jazə 'dakə ...?]
It's OK.	**Nu face nimic.** [nu 'faʧe ni'mik]
It's all right.	**Este în regulă.** [este in 'regulə]
Don't worry about it.	**Nu aveţi pentru ce.** [nu a'vets^j 'pentru ʧe]

Agreement

Yes.	**Da.** [da]
Yes, sure.	**Da, desigur.** [da, de'sigur]
OK (Good!)	**Bine!** ['bine!]
Very well.	**Foarte bine.** [fo'arte 'bine]
Certainly!	**Cu siguranţă!** [ku sigu'rantse!]
I agree.	**Sunt de acord.** [sunt de a'kord]
That's correct.	**Corect.** [ko'rekt]
That's right.	**Aşa e.** [a'ʃa e]
You're right.	**Ai dreptate.** [aj drep'tate]
I don't mind.	**Nu mă deranjează.** [nu mə deran'ʒ'azə]
Absolutely right.	**Fix aşa.** [fiks aʃa]
It's possible.	**Poate.** [po'ate]
That's a good idea.	**E o idee bună.** [e o i'dee 'bunə]
I can't say no.	**Nu pot să refuz.** [nu pot sə re'fuz]
I'd be happy to.	**Mi-ar face plăcere.** [mi-ar 'fatʃe plə'tʃere]
With pleasure.	**Cu plăcere.** [ku plə'tʃere]

Refusal. Expressing doubt

No.	**Nu.** [nu]
Certainly not.	**Cu siguranță nu.** [ku sigu'rantsə nu]
I don't agree.	**Nu sunt de acord.** [nu sunt de a'kord]
I don't think so.	**Nu cred.** [nu kred]
It's not true.	**Nu e adevărat.** [nu e adevə'rat]
You are wrong.	**Vă înşelaţi.** [və înʃe'latsʲ]
I think you are wrong.	**Cred că faceţi o greşeală.** [kred tʃe 'fatʃetsʲ o gre'ʃʲalə]
I'm not sure.	**Nu sunt sigur.** [nu sunt si'gur /si'gurə/]
It's impossible.	**Este imposibil.** [este impo'sibil]
Nothing of the kind (sort)!	**Nici vorbă!** [nitʃi 'vorbə!]
The exact opposite.	**Exact pe dos.** [e'gzakt pe dos]
I'm against it.	**Sunt împotrivă.** [sunt împo'trivə]
I don't care.	**Nu-mi pasă.** [nu-mi 'pasə]
I have no idea.	**Nu am idee.** [nu am i'dee]
I doubt it.	**Mă cam îndoiesc.** [mə kam îndo'jesk]
Sorry, I can't.	**Îmi pare rău, nu pot.** [îmʲ 'pare rəu, nu pot]
Sorry, I don't want to.	**Îmi pare rău, nu vreau.** [îmʲ 'pare rəu, nu 'vrʲau]
Thank you, but I don't need this.	**Mulţumesc dar nu am nevoie.** [multsu'mesk dar nu am ne'voje]
It's getting late.	**Se face târziu.** [se 'fatʃe tîr'zju]

I have to get up early.

Trebuie să mă trezesc devreme.
[trebuje sə mə tre'zesk de'vreme]

I don't feel well.

Nu mă simt bine.
[nu mə simt 'bine]

Expressing gratitude

Thank you.	**Mulțumesc.** [mulʦu'mesk]
Thank you very much.	**Vă mulțumesc foarte mult.** [və mulʦu'mesk fo'arte mult]
I really appreciate it.	**Mulțumesc frumos.** [mulʦu'mesk fru'mos /frumo'asə/]
I'm really grateful to you.	**Vă sunt recunoscător /recunoscătoare/.** [və sunt rekunoskə'tor /rekunoskəto'are/]
We are really grateful to you.	**Vă suntem recunoscători.** [və 'suntem rekunoskə'tori]
Thank you for your time.	**Vă mulțumesc pentru timpul acordat.** [və mulʦu'mesk 'pentru 'timpul akor'dat]
Thanks for everything.	**Mulțumesc pentru tot.** [mulʦu'mesk 'pentru tot]
Thank you for ...	**Mulțumesc pentru ...** [mulʦu'mesk 'pentru ...]
your help	**ajutor** [aʒu'tor]
a nice time	**timpul petrecut împreună** [timpul petre'kut imprə'unə]
a wonderful meal	**o masă excelentă** [o 'masə ekstʃe'lentə]
a pleasant evening	**o seară plăcută** [o 'sʲarə plə'kutə]
a wonderful day	**o zi minunată** [o zi minu'natə]
an amazing journey	**o călătorie extraordinară** [o kələto'rie ekstraordi'narə]
Don't mention it.	**Nu aveți pentru ce.** [nu a'vetsʲ 'pentru tʃe]
You are welcome.	**Cu plăcere.** [ku plə'tʃere]
Any time.	**Oricând.** [ori'kind]
My pleasure.	**Plăcerea este de partea mea.** [plə'tʃerʲa 'este de 'partʲa mʲa]

Forget it.	**N-ai pentru ce.**
[naj 'pentru t͡ʃe]

Don't worry about it.	**Pentru puțin.**
[pentru put'sin]

Congratulations. Best wishes

Congratulations!

Felicitări!
[felitʃi'tɛri!]

Happy birthday!

La mulți ani!
[la 'mulʦʲ anʲ!]

Merry Christmas!

Crăciun fericit!
[krə'ʧiun feri'ʧit!]

Happy New Year!

Un An Nou fericit!
[un an nou feri'ʧit!]

Happy Easter!

Paşte fericit!
[paʃte feri'ʧit!]

Happy Hanukkah!

Hanuka fericită!
[hanuka feri'ʧitə!]

I'd like to propose a toast.

Aş dori să închin în toast.
[aʃ do'ri sə ɨn'kin ɨn tost]

Cheers!

Noroc!
[no'rok!]

Let's drink to ...!

Să bem pentru ...!
[sə bem 'pentru ...!]

To our success!

Pentru succesul nostru!
[pentru suk'ʧesul 'nostru!]

To your success!

Pentru succesul dumneavoastră!
[pentru suk'ʧesul dumnʲavo'astrə!]

Good luck!

Baftă!
['baftə!]

Have a nice day!

Să aveți o zi frumoasă!
[sə a'vetsʲ o zi frumo'asə!]

Have a good holiday!

Vacanță plăcută!
[va'kanʦə plə'kutə!]

Have a safe journey!

Drum bun!
[drum bun!]

I hope you get better soon!

Multă sănătate!
[multə sənə'tate!]

Socializing

Why are you sad?	**De ce eşti supărat /supărată/?** [de tʃe 'eʃtʲ supə'rat /supə'ratə/?]
Smile! Cheer up!	**Zâmbeşte!** [zɨm'beʃte!]
Are you free tonight?	**Eşti liber /liberă/ în seara asta?** [eʃtʲ 'liber /'liberə/ ɨn 'sʲara 'asta?]

May I offer you a drink?	**Pot să îţi fac cinste cu o băutură?** [pot sə 'ɨtsʲ fak 'tʃinste ku o bəu'turə?]
Would you like to dance?	**Vrei să dansezi?** [vrej sə dan'sezi?]
Let's go to the movies.	**Hai să mergem la film.** [haj sə 'merdʒem la film]

May I invite you to ...?	**Pot să te invit la ...?** [pot sə te in'vit la ...?]
a restaurant	**un restaurant** [un restau'rant]
the movies	**film** [film]
the theater	**teatru** [te'atru]
go for a walk	**o plimbare** [o plim'bare]

At what time?	**La ce oră?** [la tʃe 'orə?]
tonight	**diseară** [di'sʲarə]
at six	**la şase** [la 'ʃase]
at seven	**la şapte** [la 'ʃapte]
at eight	**la opt** [la opt]
at nine	**la nouă** [la 'nowə]

Do you like it here?	**Îţi place aici?** [ɨtsʲ 'platʃie a'itʃi?]
Are you here with someone?	**Eşti cu cineva?** [eʃtʲ ku tʃine'va?]
I'm with my friend.	**Sunt cu un prieten /o prietenă/.** [sunt ku un pri'eten /o pri'etenə/]

I'm with my friends. | **Sunt cu niște prieteni.**
[sunt ku 'niʃte pri'etenj]

No, I'm alone. | **Nu, sunt singur /singură/.**
[nu, sunt 'singur /'singurə/]

Do you have a boyfriend? | **Ai prieten?**
[aj pri'eten?]

I have a boyfriend. | **Am prieten.**
[am pri'eten]

Do you have a girlfriend? | **Ai prietenă?**
[aj pri'etenə?]

I have a girlfriend. | **Am prietenă.**
[am pri'etenə]

Can I see you again? | **Pot să te mai văd?**
[pot sə te maj vəd?]

Can I call you? | **Pot să te sun?**
[pot sə te sun?]

Call me. (Give me a call.) | **Sună-mă.**
['sunə-mə]

What's your number? | **Care este numărul tău de telefon?**
[kare 'este 'numərul təu de tele'fon?]

I miss you. | **Mi-e dor de tine.**
[mi-e dor de 'tine]

You have a beautiful name. | **Ce nume frumos ai.**
[tʃe 'nume 'frumos aj]

I love you. | **Te iubesc.**
[te ju'besk]

Will you marry me? | **Vrei să fii soția mea?**
[vrej sə fii sot'sia mʲa?]

You're kidding! | **Glumești!**
[glu'meʃti!]

I'm just kidding. | **Glumeam.**
[glu'mʲam]

Are you serious? | **Vorbiți serios?**
[vor'bitsʲ se'rjos?]

I'm serious. | **Vorbesc serios.**
[vor'besk se'rjos]

Really?! | **Serios?!**
[se'rjos?!]

It's unbelievable! | **Incredibil!**
[inkre'dibil!]

I don't believe you. | **Nu vă cred.**
[nu və kred]

I can't. | **Nu pot.**
[nu pot]

I don't know. | **Nu știu.**
[nu 'ʃtiu]

I don't understand you. | **Nu vă înțeleg.**
[nu və intse'leg]

Please go away.

Vă rog să plecați.
[və rog sə ple'katsʲ]

Leave me alone!

Lăsați-mă în pace!
[lə'satsi-mə ɨn 'patʃe!]

I can't stand him.

Nu pot să îl sufăr.
[nu pot sə ɨl 'sufər]

You are disgusting!

Sunteți enervant!
[sun'tetsʲ ener'vant!]

I'll call the police!

Chem poliția!
[kem po'litsʲa!]

Sharing impressions. Emotions

I like it.	**Îmi place.** [ɨmʲ ˈplaʧe]
Very nice.	**Foarte drăguţ.** [foˈarte drəˈguʦ]
That's great!	**Minunat!** [minuˈnat!]
It's not bad.	**Nu e rău.** [nu e rəu]
I don't like it.	**Nu îmi place.** [nu ɨmj ˈplaʧe]
It's not good.	**Nu e bine.** [nu e ˈbine]
It's bad.	**E grav.** [e grav]
It's very bad.	**E foarte grav.** [e foˈarte grav]
It's disgusting.	**E dezgustător.** [e dezgustəˈtor]
I'm happy.	**Sunt fericit /fericită/.** [sunt feriˈʧit /feriˈʧitə/]
I'm content.	**Sunt mulţumit /mulţumită/.** [sunt mulʦuˈmit /mulʦuˈmitə/]
I'm in love.	**Sunt îndrăgostit /îndrăgostită/.** [sunt ɨndrəgosˈtit /ɨndrəgosˈtitə/]
I'm calm.	**Sunt calm /calmă/.** [sunt kalm /ˈkalmə/]
I'm bored.	**Mă plictisesc.** [mə pliktiˈsesk]
I'm tired.	**Sunt obosit /obosită/.** [sunt oboˈsit /oboˈsitə/]
I'm sad.	**Sunt trist /tristă/.** [sunt trist /ˈtristə/]
I'm frightened.	**Mi-e frică.** [mi-e ˈfrikə]
I'm angry.	**Sunt nervos /nervoasă/.** [sunt nerˈvos /nervoˈasə/]
I'm worried.	**Sunt îngrijorat /îngrijorată/.** [sunt ɨngriʒoˈrat /ɨngriʒoˈratə/]
I'm nervous.	**Sunt neliniştit /neliniştită/.** [sunt neliniʃˈtit /neliniʃˈtitə/]

I'm jealous. (envious)

Sunt gelos /geloasă/.
[sunt ʤe'los /ʤelo'asə/]

I'm surprised.

Sunt surprins /surprinsă/.
[sunt sur'prins /sur'prinsə/]

I'm perplexed.

Sunt nedumerit /nedumerită/.
[sunt nedume'rit /nedume'ritə/]

Problems. Accidents

I've got a problem.

Am o problemă.
[am o pro'blemə]

We've got a problem.

Avem o problemă.
[a'vem o pro'blemə]

I'm lost.

M-am rătăcit.
[mam rətə'tʃit]

I missed the last bus (train).

Am pierdut ultimul autobuz (tren).
[am 'pjerdut 'ultimul auto'buz (tren)]

I don't have any money left.

Am rămas fără niciun ban.
[am rə'mas 'fərə 'nitʃiun ban]

I've lost my ...

Mi-am pierdut ...
[mi-am 'pjerdut ...]

Someone stole my ...

Cineva mi-a furat ...
[tʃine'va mi-a fu'rat ...]

passport

paşaportul
[paʃa'portul]

wallet

portofelul
[porto'felul]

papers

actele
['aktele]

ticket

biletul
[bi'letul]

money

banii
['banii]

handbag

geanta
[dʒanta]

camera

aparat (n) foto
[apa'rat 'foto]

laptop

laptopul
[ləp'topul]

tablet computer

tableta
[tab'leta]

mobile phone

telefonul mobil
[tele'fonul mo'bil]

Help me!

Ajutaţi-mă!
[aʒu'tatsi-mə!]

What's happened?

Ce s-a întâmplat?
[tʃe sa intim'plat?]

fire

incendiu
[in'tʃendju]

shooting	**împuşcături** [împuʃke'turi]
murder	**crimă** ['krimə]
explosion	**explozie** [eks'plozie]
fight	**luptă** ['luptə]

Call the police!	**Chemaţi poliţia!** [ke'matsʲ po'litsja!]
Please hurry up!	**Grabiţi-vă, vă rog!** [gra'bitsi-ve, ve rog!]
I'm looking for the police station.	**Caut secţia de poliţie.** [kaut 'sektsja de po'litsje]
I need to make a call.	**Trebuie să dau un telefon.** [trebuje se dau un tele'fon]
May I use your phone?	**Pot folosi telefonul dumneavoastră?** [pot folo'si tele'fonul dumnʲavo'astre?]

I've been ...	**Am fost ...** [am fost ...]
mugged	**tâlhărit /tâlhărită/** [tɨlhe'rit /tɨlhe'ritə/]
robbed	**jefuit /jefuită/** [ʒefu'it /ʒefu'ite/]
raped	**violată** [vio'late]
attacked (beaten up)	**atacat /atacată/** [ata'kat /ata'kate/]

Are you all right?	**Sunteţi bine?** [sun'tetsʲ 'bine?]
Did you see who it was?	**Aţi văzut cine era?** [atsʲ ve'zut tʃine e'ra?]
Would you be able to recognize the person?	**Aţi fi în stare să recunoaşteţi făptaşul?** [atsʲ fi ɨn 'stare se re'kunoaʃtetsi fepta'ʃul?]
Are you sure?	**Sunteţi sigur /sigură/?** [sun'tetsʲ 'sigur /'sigure/?]

Please calm down.	**Vă rog să vă calmaţi.** [ve rog se ve kal'matsʲ]
Take it easy!	**Liniştiţi-vă!** [lini'ʃtitsi-ve!]
Don't worry!	**Nu vă faceţi griji!** [nu ve 'fatʃetsʲ griʒʲ!]
Everything will be fine.	**Totul va fi bine.** [totul va fi 'bine]
Everything's all right.	**Totul este în regulă.** [totul 'este ɨn 'regule]

Come here, please.	**Veniți aici, vă rog.** [ve'nițsi a'itʃi, və rog]
I have some questions for you.	**Am câteva întrebări pentru dumneavoastră.** [am kite'va intre'bɛrj 'pentru dumn'avo'astrə]
Wait a moment, please.	**Așteptați o clipă, vă rog.** [aʃtep'tatsʲ o 'klipə, və rog]
Do you have any I.D.?	**Aveți vreun act de identitate?** [a'vetsʲ 'vreun akt de identi'tate?]
Thanks. You can leave now.	**Mulțumesc. Puteți pleca acum.** [mulʦu'mesk. Pu'tetsʲ ple'ka a'kum]
Hands behind your head!	**Mâinile la ceafă!** [mɨjnile la 'tʃafə!]
You're under arrest!	**Sunteți arestat /arestată/!** [sun'tetsʲ ares'tat /ares'tatə/!]

Health problems

Please help me.	**Vă rog să mă ajutați.** [və rog sə mə aʒu'taʦʲ]
I don't feel well.	**Mi-e rău.** [mi-e 'rəu]
My husband doesn't feel well.	**Soțului meu îi este rău.** [soʦului 'meu ɨi 'este rəu]
My son ...	**Fiului meu ...** [fjului 'meu ...]
My father ...	**Tatălui meu ...** [tatəlui 'meu ...]
My wife doesn't feel well.	**Soției mele îi este rău.** [so'ʦiej 'mele ɨi 'este rəu]
My daughter ...	**Fiicei mele ...** [fiiʧej 'mele ...]
My mother ...	**Mamei mele ...** [mamej 'mele ...]
I've got a ...	**Mă doare ...** [mə do'are ...]
headache	**capul** ['kapul]
sore throat	**în gât** [ɨn gɨt]
stomach ache	**stomacul** [sto'makul]
toothache	**o măsea** [o mə'sʲa]
I feel dizzy.	**Sunt amețit /amețită/.** [sunt ame'ʦit /ame'ʦitə/]
He has a fever.	**El are febră.** [el are 'febrə]
She has a fever.	**Ea are febră.** [ja are 'febrə]
I can't breathe.	**Nu pot să respir.** [nu pot sə res'pir]
I'm short of breath.	**Respir greu.** [res'pir 'greu]
I am asthmatic.	**Am astm.** [am astm]
I am diabetic.	**Am diabet.** [am dia'bet]

I can't sleep.
Nu pot să form.
[nu pot sə form]

food poisoning
intoxicaţie alimentară
[intoksi'katsie alimen'tarə]

It hurts here.
Mă doare aici.
[mə do'are a'itʃi]

Help me!
Ajutor!
[aʒu'tor!]

I am here!
Sunt aici!
[sunt a'itʃi!]

We are here!
Suntem aici!
[suntem a'itʃi!]

Get me out of here!
Scoateţi-mă de aici!
[skoa'tetsi-mə de a'itʃi!]

I need a doctor.
Am nevoie de un doctor.
[am ne'voje de un dok'tor]

I can't move.
Nu pot să mă mişc.
[nu pot sə mə miʃk]

I can't move my legs.
Nu îmi pot mişca picioarele.
[nu imj pot 'miʃka pitʃio'arele]

I have a wound.
Sunt rănit /rănită/.
[sunt rə'nit /rə'nitə/]

Is it serious?
Este grav?
[este grav?]

My documents are in my pocket.
Actele mele sunt în buzunar.
[aktele 'mele sunt in buzu'nar]

Calm down!
Calmaţi-vă!
[kal'matsi-və!]

May I use your phone?
Pot folosi telefonul dumneavoastră?
[pot folo'si tele'fonul dumnʲavo'astrə?]

Call an ambulance!
Chemaţi o ambulanţă!
[ke'matsʲ o ambu'lantsə!]

It's urgent!
Este urgent!
[este ur'dʒent!]

It's an emergency!
Este o urgenţă!
[este o ur'dʒentsə!]

Please hurry up!
Grabiţi-vă, vă rog!
[gra'bitsi-və, və rog!]

Would you please call a doctor?
Vreţi să chemaţi un doctor?
[vretsʲ sə ke'matsʲ un 'doktor?]

Where is the hospital?
Unde este spitalul?
[unde 'este spi'talul?]

How are you feeling?
Cum vă simţiţi?
[kum və sim'tsitsʲ?]

Are you all right?
Sunteţi bine?
[sun'tetsʲ 'bine?]

What's happened?
Ce s-a întâmplat?
[tʃe sa intim'plat?]

I feel better now.

Mă simt mai bine acum.
[mə simt maj 'bine a'kum]

It's OK.

E bine.
[e 'bine]

It's all right.

E în regulă.
[e ɨn 'regulə]

At the pharmacy

pharmacy (drugstore)	**farmacie** [farma'ʧie]
24-hour pharmacy	**farmacie non-stop** [farma'ʧie non-stop]
Where is the closest pharmacy?	**Unde este cea mai apropiată farmacie?** [unde 'este ʧa maj apro'pjatə farma'ʧie?]
Is it open now?	**Este deschis acum?** [este des'kis a'kum?]
At what time does it open?	**La ce oră deschide?** [la ʧe 'orə des'kide?]
At what time does it close?	**La ce oră închide?** [la ʧe 'orə in'kide?]
Is it far?	**Este departe?** [este de'parte?]
Can I get there on foot?	**Pot merge pe jos până acolo?** [pot 'merʤe pe ʒos 'pinə a'kolo?]
Can you show me on the map?	**Îmi puteți arăta pe hartă?** [imʲ pu'tetsʲ arə'ta pe 'hartə?]
Please give me something for ...	**Vă rog să îmi dați ceva pentru ...** [və rog sə imʲ 'datsʲ ʧe'va 'pentru ...]
a headache	**durere de cap** [du'rere de kap]
a cough	**tuse** ['tuse]
a cold	**răceală** [rə'ʧalə]
the flu	**gripă** ['gripə]
a fever	**febră** ['febrə]
a stomach ache	**durere de stomac** [du'rere de sto'mak]
nausea	**greață** [grʲatsə]
diarrhea	**diaree** [dia'ree]
constipation	**constipație** [konsti'patsie]

pain in the back

durere de spate
[du'rere de 'spate]

chest pain

durere în piept
[du'rere in pjept]

side stitch

junghi lateral
[ʒungʲ late'ral]

abdominal pain

durere abdominală
[du'rere abdomi'nale]

---

pill

pastilă
[pas'tile]

ointment, cream

unguent, cremă
[ungu'ent, 'kreme]

syrup

sirop
[si'rop]

spray

spray
[spraj]

drops

dropsuri
[dropsurʲ]

You need to go to the hospital.

Trebuie să mergeți la spital.
[trebuje se mer'dʒetsʲ la spi'tal]

health insurance

asigurare de sănătate
[asigu'rare de sene'tate]

prescription

rețetă
[re'tsete]

insect repellant

produs anti insecte
[pro'dus 'anti in'sekte]

Band Aid

plasture
['plasture]

The bare minimum

Excuse me, ...	**Nu vă supărați, ...** [nu və supǝ'rats, ...]
Hello.	**Buna ziua.** [buna 'ziwa]
Thank you.	**Mulțumesc.** [mulʦu'mesk]
Good bye.	**La revedere.** [la reve'dere]
Yes.	**Da.** [da]
No.	**Nu.** [nu]
I don't know.	**Nu știu.** [nu 'ʃtiu]
Where? | Where to? | When?	**Unde? | Încotro? | Când?** [unde? | ɨnko'tro? | kɨnd?]
I need ...	**Am nevoie de ...** [am ne'voje de ...]
I want ...	**Vreau ...** [vr'au ...]
Do you have ...?	**Aveți ...?** [a'vets ...?]
Is there a ... here?	**Există ... aici?** [e'gziste ... a'itʃi?]
May I ...?	**Pot ...?** [pot ...?]
..., please (polite request)	**..., vă rog** [..., vǝ rog]
I'm looking for ...	**Caut ...** [kaut ...]
the restroom	**o toaletă** [o toa'letǝ]
an ATM	**un bancomat** [un banko'mat]
a pharmacy (drugstore)	**o farmacie** [o farma'ʧie]
a hospital	**un spital** [un spi'tal]
the police station	**o secție de poliție** [o 'sekʦie de po'liʦie]
the subway	**un metrou** [un me'trou]

a taxi	**un taxi** [un ta'ksi]
the train station	**o gară** [o 'garə]

My name is ...	**Numele meu este ...** [numele 'meu 'este ...]
What's your name?	**Cum vă numiți?** [kum və nu'mitsʲ?]
Could you please help me?	**Mă puteți ajuta, vă rog?** [mə pu'tetsʲ aʒu'ta, və rog?]
I've got a problem.	**Am o problemă.** [am o pro'blemə]
I don't feel well.	**Mi-e rău.** [mi-e 'rəu]
Call an ambulance!	**Chemați o ambulanță!** [ke'matsʲ o ambu'lantsə!]
May I make a call?	**Pot să dau un telefon?** [pot sə dau un tele'fon?]

I'm sorry.	**Îmi pare rău.** [ɨmʲ 'pare rəu]
You're welcome.	**Cu plăcere.** [ku plə'tʃere]

I, me	**Eu** [eu]
you (inform.)	**tu** [tu]
he	**el** [el]
she	**ea** [ja]
they (masc.)	**ei** [ej]
they (fem.)	**ele** ['ele]
we	**noi** [noj]
you (pl)	**voi** [voj]
you (sg, form.)	**dumneavoastră** [dumnʲavo'astrə]

ENTRANCE	**INTRARE** [in'trare]
EXIT	**IEȘIRE** [je'ʃire]
OUT OF ORDER	**DEFECT** [de'fekt]
CLOSED	**ÎNCHIS** [ɨn'kis]

OPEN

DESCHIS
[des'kis]

FOR WOMEN

PENTRU FEMEI
[pentru fe'mej]

FOR MEN

PENTRU BĂRBAȚI
[pentru bər'batsʲ]

TOPICAL VOCABULARY

This section contains more than 3,000 of the most important words.
The dictionary will provide invaluable assistance while traveling abroad, because frequently individual words are enough for you to be understood.
The dictionary includes a convenient transcription of each foreign word

T&P Books Publishing

VOCABULARY
CONTENTS

T&P Books Publishing

BASIC CONCEPTS

T&P Books Publishing

1. Pronouns

I, me	**eu**	[eu]
you	**tu**	[tu]
he	**el**	[el]
she	**ea**	[ʲa]
we	**noi**	[noj]
you (to a group)	**voi**	['voj]
they (masc.)	**ei**	['ej]
they (fem.)	**ele**	['ele]

2. Greetings. Salutations

Hello! (fam.)	**Bună ziua!**	['bune 'ziwa]
Hello! (form.)	**Bună ziua!**	['bune 'ziwa]
Good morning!	**Bună dimineața!**	['bune dimi'nʲatsa]
Good afternoon!	**Bună ziua!**	['bune 'ziwa]
Good evening!	**Bună seara!**	['bune 'sʲara]
to say hello	**a se saluta**	[a se salu'ta]
Hi! (hello)	**Salut!**	[sa'lut]
greeting (n)	**salut** (n)	[sa'lut]
to greet (vt)	**a saluta**	[a salu'ta]
How are you?	**Ce mai faci?**	[tʃie maj 'fatʃi]
What's new?	**Ce mai e nou?**	[tʃe maj e 'nou]
Bye-Bye! Goodbye!	**La revedere!**	[la reve'dere]
See you soon!	**Pe curând!**	[pe ku'rind]
Farewell! (to a friend)	**Rămâi cu bine!**	[rə'mij ku 'bine]
Farewell! (form.)	**Rămâneți cu bine!**	[rəmiʲ'nets ku 'bine]
to say goodbye	**a-și lua rămas bun**	[aʃ lu'a rə'mas bun]
So long!	**Pa!**	[pa]
Thank you!	**Mulțumesc!**	[multsu'mesk]
Thank you very much!	**Mulțumesc mult!**	[multsu'mesk mult]
You're welcome	**Cu plăcere**	[ku plə'tʃere]
Don't mention it!	**Pentru puțin**	['pentru pu'tsin]
It was nothing	**Pentru puțin**	['pentru pu'tsin]
Excuse me! (fam.)	**Scuză-mă!**	['skuzəmə]
Excuse me! (form.)	**Scuzați-mă!**	[sku'zatsimə]
to excuse (forgive)	**a scuza**	[a sku'za]

to apologize (vi)	a cere scuze	[a 'ʧere 'skuze]
My apologies	Cer scuze	[ʧer 'skuze]
I'm sorry!	Lertaţi-mă!	[er'taʦimə]
to forgive (vt)	a ierta	[a er'ta]
please (adv)	vă rog	[və rog]
Don't forget!	Nu uitaţi!	[nu uj'taʦʲ]
Certainly!	Desigur!	[de'sigur]
Of course not!	Desigur ca nu!	[de'sigur kə nu]
Okay! (I agree)	Sunt de acord!	[sunt de a'kord]
That's enough!	Ajunge!	[a'ʒunʤe]

<h2>3. Questions</h2>

Who?	Cine?	['ʧine]
What?	Ce?	[ʧe]
Where? (at, in)	Unde?	['unde]
Where (to)?	Unde?	['unde]
From where?	De unde?	[de 'unde]
When?	Când?	[kind]
Why? (What for?)	Pentru ce?	['pentru ʧe]
Why? (~ are you crying?)	De ce?	[de ʧe]
What for?	Pentru ce?	['pentru ʧe]
How? (in what way)	Cum?	[kum]
What? (What kind of ...?)	Care?	['kare]
Which?	Care?	['kare]
To whom?	Cui?	[kuj]
About whom?	Despre cine?	['despre 'ʧine]
About what?	Despre ce?	['despre ʧe]
With whom?	Cu cine?	[ku 'ʧine]
How many?	Cât? Câtă?	[kit], ['kitə]
How much?	Câţi? Câte?	[kiʦ], ['kite]
Whose?	Al cui?	['al kuj]
Whose? (fem.)	A cui?	[a kuj]
Whose? (pl)	Ai cui?, Ale cui?	[aj kuj], ['ale kuj]

<h2>4. Prepositions</h2>

with (accompanied by)	cu	[ku]
without	fără	[fərə]
to (indicating direction)	la	[la]
about (talking ~ ...)	despre	['despre]
before (in time)	înainte de	[ɨna'inte de]
in front of ...	înaintea	[ɨna'intʲa]
under (beneath, below)	sub	[sub]

above (over)	deasupra	[dʲa'supra]
on (atop)	pe	[pe]
from (off, out of)	din	[din]
of (made from)	din	[din]

| in (e.g., ~ ten minutes) | peste | ['peste] |
| over (across the top of) | prin | [prin] |

5. Function words. Adverbs. Part 1

Where? (at, in)	Unde?	['unde]
here (adv)	aici	[a'iʧi]
there (adv)	acolo	[a'kolo]

| somewhere (to be) | undeva | [unde'va] |
| nowhere (not in any place) | nicăieri | [nikə'erʲ] |

| by (near, beside) | lângă ... | ['lɨngə] |
| by the window | lângă fereastră | ['lɨngə fe'rʲastrə] |

Where (to)?	Unde?	['unde]
here (e.g., come ~!)	aici	[a'iʧi]
there (e.g., to go ~)	acolo	[a'kolo]
from here (adv)	de aici	[de a'iʧi]
from there (adv)	de acolo	[de a'kolo]

| close (adv) | aproape | [apro'ape] |
| far (adv) | departe | [de'parte] |

near (e.g., ~ Paris)	alături	[a'ləturʲ]
nearby (adv)	alături	[a'ləturʲ]
not far (adv)	aproape	[apro'ape]

left (adj)	stâng	[stɨng]
on the left	din stânga	[din 'stɨnga]
to the left	în stânga	[ɨn 'stɨnga]

right (adj)	drept	[drept]
on the right	din dreapta	[din 'drʲapta]
to the right	în dreapta	[ɨn 'drʲapta]

in front (adv)	în faţă	[ɨn 'fatsə]
front (as adj)	din faţă	[din 'fatsə]
ahead (the kids ran ~)	înainte	[ina'inte]

behind (adv)	în urmă	[ɨn 'urmə]
from behind	din spate	[din 'spate]
back (towards the rear)	înapoi	[ina'poj]
middle	mijloc (n)	['miʒlok]
in the middle	la mijloc	[la 'miʒlok]

at the side	dintr-o parte	['dintro 'parte]
everywhere (adv)	peste tot	['peste tot]
around (in all directions)	în jur	[ɨn ʒur]

from inside	dinăuntru	[dinə'untru]
somewhere (to go)	undeva	[unde'va]
straight (directly)	direct	[di'rekt]
back (e.g., come ~)	înapoi	[ɨna'poj]

| from anywhere | de undeva | [de unde'va] |
| from somewhere | de undeva | [de unde'va] |

firstly (adv)	în primul rând	[ɨn 'primul rɨnd]
secondly (adv)	în al doilea rând	[ɨn al 'dojlʲa rɨnd]
thirdly (adv)	în al treilea rând	[ɨn al 'trejlʲa rɨnd]

suddenly (adv)	deodată	[deo'datə]
at first (in the beginning)	la început	[la ɨnt͡ʃe'put]
for the first time	prima dată	['prima 'datə]
long before …	cu mult timp	[ku mult timp
	înainte de …	ɨna'inte de]
anew (over again)	din nou	[din 'nou]
for good (adv)	pentru totdeauna	['pentru totdʲa'una]

never (adv)	niciodată	[nit͡ʃio'datə]
again (adv)	iarăşi	['jarəʃ]
now (at present)	acum	[a'kum]
often (adv)	des	[des]
then (adv)	atunci	[a'tunt͡ʃi]
urgently (quickly)	urgent	[ur'dʒent]
usually (adv)	de obicei	[de obi't͡ʃej]

by the way, …	apropo	[apro'po]
possibly	posibil	[po'sibil]
probably (adv)	probabil	[pro'babil]
maybe (adv)	poate	[po'ate]
besides …	în afară de aceasta, …	[ɨn a'farə de a't͡ʃasta]
that's why …	de aceea	[de a't͡ʃeja]
in spite of …	deşi …	[de'ʃi]
thanks to …	datorită …	[dato'ritə]

what (pron.)	ce	[t͡ʃe]
that (conj.)	că	[kə]
something	ceva	[t͡ʃe'va]
anything (something)	ceva	[t͡ʃe'va]
nothing	nimic	[ni'mik]

who (pron.)	cine	['t͡ʃine]
someone	cineva	[t͡ʃine'va]
somebody	cineva	[t͡ʃine'va]
nobody	nimeni	['nimenʲ]
nowhere (a voyage to ~)	nicăieri	[nikə'erʲ]

| nobody's | al nimănui | [al nime'nuj] |
| somebody's | al cuiva | [al kuj'va] |

so (I'm ~ glad)	aşa	[a'ʃa]
also (as well)	de asemenea	[de a'semenia]
too (as well)	la fel	[la fel]

6. Function words. Adverbs. Part 2

Why?	De ce?	[de ʧe]
for some reason	nu se ştie de ce	[nu se 'ʃtie de ʧe]
because ...	pentru că ...	['pentru kə]
for some purpose	cine ştie pentru ce	['ʧine 'ʃtie 'pentru ʧe]

and	şi	[ʃi]
or	sau	['sau]
but	dar	[dar]
for (e.g., ~ me)	pentru	['pentru]

too (~ many people)	prea	[pria]
only (exclusively)	numai	['numaj]
exactly (adv)	exact	[e'gzakt]
about (more or less)	vreo	['vreo]

approximately (adv)	aproximativ	[aproksima'tiv]
approximate (adj)	aproximativ	[aproksima'tiv]
almost (adv)	aproape	[apro'ape]
the rest	restul	['restul]

each (adj)	fiecare	[fie'kare]
any (no matter which)	oricare	[ori'kare]
many, much (a lot of)	mult	[mult]
many people	mulţi	[mulʦ]
all (everyone)	toţi	[toʦ]

in return for ...	în schimb la ...	[ɨn 'skimb la]
in exchange (adv)	în schimbul	[ɨn 'skimbul]
by hand (made)	manual	[manu'al]
hardly (negative opinion)	puţin probabil	[pu'ʦin pro'babil]

probably (adv)	probabil	[pro'babil]
on purpose (intentionally)	intenţionat	[intenʦio'nat]
by accident (adv)	întâmplător	[ɨntɨmplə'tor]

very (adv)	foarte	[fo'arte]
for example (adv)	de exemplu	[de e'gzemplu]
between	între	['ɨntre]
among	printre	['printre]
so much (such a lot)	atât	[a'tɨt]
especially (adv)	mai ales	[maj a'les]

NUMBERS.
MISCELLANEOUS

T&P Books Publishing

0 zero	**zero**	['zero]
1 one	**unu**	['unu]
2 two	**doi**	[doj]
3 three	**trei**	[trej]
4 four	**patru**	['patru]
5 five	**cinci**	[ʧinʧ]
6 six	**şase**	['ʃase]
7 seven	**şapte**	['ʃapte]
8 eight	**opt**	[opt]
9 nine	**nouă**	['nowə]
10 ten	**zece**	['zeʧe]
11 eleven	**unsprezece**	['unsprezeʧe]
12 twelve	**doisprezece**	['dojsprezeʧe]
13 thirteen	**treisprezece**	['trejsprezeʧe]
14 fourteen	**paisprezece**	['pajsprezeʧe]
15 fifteen	**cincisprezece**	['ʧinʧsprezeʧe]
16 sixteen	**şaisprezece**	['ʃajsprezeʧe]
17 seventeen	**şaptesprezece**	['ʃaptesprezeʧe]
18 eighteen	**optsprezece**	['optsprezeʧe]
19 nineteen	**nouăsprezece**	['nowəsprezeʧe]
20 twenty	**douăzeci**	[dowe'zeʧi]
21 twenty-one	**douăzeci şi unu**	[dowe'zeʧi ʃi 'unu]
22 twenty-two	**douăzeci şi doi**	[dowe'zeʧi ʃi doj]
23 twenty-three	**douăzeci şi trei**	[dowe'zeʧi ʃi trej]
30 thirty	**treizeci**	[trej'zeʧi]
31 thirty-one	**treizeci şi unu**	[trej'zeʧi ʃi 'unu]
32 thirty-two	**treizeci şi doi**	[trej'zeʧi ʃi doj]
33 thirty-three	**treizeci şi trei**	[trej'zeʧi ʃi trej]
40 forty	**patruzeci**	[patru'zeʧi]
41 forty-one	**patruzeci şi unu**	[patru'zeʧi ʃi 'unu]
42 forty-two	**patruzeci şi doi**	[patru'zeʧi ʃi doj]
43 forty-three	**patruzeci şi trei**	[patru'zeʧi ʃi trej]
50 fifty	**cincizeci**	[ʧinʧ'zeʧ]
51 fifty-one	**cincizeci şi unu**	[ʧinʧ'zeʧ ʃi 'unu]
52 fifty-two	**cincizeci şi doi**	[ʧinʧ'zeʧ ʃi doj]
53 fifty-three	**cincizeci şi trei**	[ʧinʧ'zeʧ ʃi trej]
60 sixty	**şaizeci**	[ʃaj'zeʧi]

61 sixty-one	şaizeci şi unu	[ʃaj'zetʃi ʃi 'unu]
62 sixty-two	şaizeci şi doi	[ʃaj'zetʃi ʃi doj]
63 sixty-three	şaizeci şi trei	[ʃaj'zetʃi ʃi trej]

70 seventy	şaptezeci	[ʃapte'zetʃi]
71 seventy-one	şaptezeci şi unu	[ʃapte'zetʃi ʃi 'unu]
72 seventy-two	şaptezeci şi doi	[ʃapte'zetʃi ʃi doj]
73 seventy-three	şaptezeci şi trei	[ʃapte'zetʃi ʃi trej]

80 eighty	optzeci	[opt'zetʃi]
81 eighty-one	optzeci şi unu	[opt'zetʃi ʃi 'unu]
82 eighty-two	optzeci şi doi	[opt'zetʃi ʃi doj]
83 eighty-three	optzeci şi trei	[opt'zetʃi ʃi trej]

90 ninety	nouăzeci	[nowə'zetʃi]
91 ninety-one	nouăzeci şi unu	[nowə'zetʃi ʃi 'unu]
92 ninety-two	nouăzeci şi doi	[nowə'zetʃi ʃi doj]
93 ninety-three	nouăzeci şi trei	[nowə'zetʃi ʃi trej]

8. Cardinal numbers. Part 2

100 one hundred	o sută	[o 'sutə]
200 two hundred	două sute	['dowə 'sute]
300 three hundred	trei sute	[trej 'sute]
400 four hundred	patru sute	['patru 'sute]
500 five hundred	cinci sute	[tʃintʃ 'sute]

600 six hundred	şase sute	['ʃase 'sute]
700 seven hundred	şapte sute	['ʃapte 'sute]
800 eight hundred	opt sute	[opt 'sute]
900 nine hundred	nouă sute	['nowə 'sute]

1000 one thousand	o mie	[o 'mie]
2000 two thousand	două mii	['dowə mij]
3000 three thousand	trei mii	[trej mij]
10000 ten thousand	zece mii	['zetʃe mij]
one hundred thousand	o sută de mii	[o 'sutə de mij]
million	milion (n)	[mi'ljon]
billion	miliard (n)	[mi'ljard]

9. Ordinal numbers

first (adj)	primul	['primul]
second (adj)	al doilea	[al 'dojlʲa]
third (adj)	al treilea	[al 'trejlʲa]
fourth (adj)	al patrulea	[al 'patrulʲa]
fifth (adj)	al cincilea	[al 'tʃintʃilʲa]
sixth (adj)	al şaselea	[al 'ʃaselʲa]

seventh (adj)	al şaptelea	[al 'ʃapteḷa]
eighth (adj)	al optulea	[al 'optuḷa]
ninth (adj)	al nouălea	[al 'nowəḷa]
tenth (adj)	al zecelea	[al 'zeʧeḷa]

COLOURS. UNITS OF MEASUREMENT

T&P Books Publishing

10. Colors

color	culoare (f)	[kulo'are]
shade (tint)	nuanță (f)	[nu'antsə]
hue	ton (n)	[ton]
rainbow	curcubeu (n)	[kurku'beu]

white (adj)	alb	[alb]
black (adj)	negru	['negru]
gray (adj)	sur	['sur]

green (adj)	verde	['verde]
yellow (adj)	galben	['galben]
red (adj)	roşu	['roʃu]
blue (adj)	albastru închis	[al'bastru i'nkis]
light blue (adj)	albastru deschis	[al'bastru des'kis]
pink (adj)	roz	['roz]
orange (adj)	portocaliu	[portoka'lju]
violet (adj)	violet	[vio'let]
brown (adj)	cafeniu	[kafe'nju]

golden (adj)	de culoarea aurului	[de kulo'arʲa 'auruluj]
silvery (adj)	argintiu	[ardʒin'tju]
beige (adj)	bej	[beʒ]
cream (adj)	crem	[krem]
turquoise (adj)	turcoaz	[turko'az]
cherry red (adj)	vişiniu	[viʃi'nju]
lilac (adj)	lila	[li'la]
crimson (adj)	de culoarea zmeurei	[de kulo'arʲa 'zmeurej]

light (adj)	de culoare deschisă	[de kulo'are des'kisə]
dark (adj)	de culoare închisă	[de kulo'are i'nkisə]
bright, vivid (adj)	aprins	[a'prins]

colored (pencils)	colorat	[kolo'rat]
color (e.g., ~ film)	color	[ko'lor]
black-and-white (adj)	alb-negru	[alb 'negru]
plain (one-colored)	monocrom	[mono'krom]
multicolored (adj)	multicolor	[multiko'lor]

11. Units of measurement

weight	greutate (f)	[greu'tate]
length	lungime (f)	[lun'dʒime]

width	**lățime** (f)	[ləˈtsime]
height	**înălțime** (f)	[inəlˈtsime]
depth	**adâncime** (f)	[adɨnˈtʃime]
volume	**volum** (n)	[voˈlum]
area	**suprafață** (f)	[supraˈfatsə]
gram	**gram** (n)	[gram]
milligram	**miligram** (n)	[miliˈgram]
kilogram	**kilogram** (n)	[kiloˈgram]
ton	**tonă** (f)	[ˈtonə]
pound	**funt** (m)	[funt]
ounce	**uncie** (f)	[ˈuntʃie]
meter	**metru** (m)	[ˈmetru]
millimeter	**milimetru** (m)	[miliˈmetru]
centimeter	**centimetru** (m)	[tʃentiˈmetru]
kilometer	**kilometru** (m)	[kiloˈmetru]
mile	**milă** (f)	[ˈmilə]
inch	**țol** (m)	[tsol]
foot	**picior** (m)	[piˈtʃior]
yard	**yard** (m)	[jard]
square meter	**metru** (m) **pătrat**	[ˈmetru pəˈtrat]
hectare	**hectar** (n)	[hekˈtar]
liter	**litru** (m)	[ˈlitru]
degree	**grad** (n)	[grad]
volt	**volt** (m)	[volt]
ampere	**amper** (m)	[amˈper]
horsepower	**cal-putere** (m)	[kal puˈtere]
quantity	**cantitate** (f)	[kantiˈtate]
a little bit of …	**puțin …**	[puˈtsin]
half	**jumătate** (f)	[ʒuməˈtate]
dozen	**duzină** (f)	[duˈzinə]
piece (item)	**bucată** (f)	[buˈkatə]
size	**dimensiune** (f)	[dimensiˈune]
scale (map ~)	**proporție** (f)	[proˈportsie]
minimal (adj)	**minim**	[ˈminim]
the smallest (adj)	**cel mai mic**	[tʃel maj mik]
medium (adj)	**de, din mijloc**	[de, din ˈmiʒlok]
maximal (adj)	**maxim**	[ˈmaksim]
the largest (adj)	**cel mai mare**	[tʃel maj ˈmare]

12. Containers

canning jar (glass ~)	**borcan** (n)	[borˈkan]
can	**cutie** (f)	[kuˈtie]

bucket	**găleată** (f)	[gə'lʲatə]
barrel	**butoi** (n)	[bu'toj]
wash basin (e.g., plastic ~)	**lighean** (n)	[li'gʲan]
tank (100L water ~)	**rezervor** (n)	[rezer'vor]
hip flask	**damigeană** (f)	[damʲ'dʒanə]
jerrycan	**canistră** (f)	[ka'nistrə]
tank (e.g., tank car)	**cisternă** (f)	[t͡ʃis'ternə]
mug	**cană** (f)	['kanə]
cup (of coffee, etc.)	**ceaşcă** (f)	['t͡ʃaʃkə]
saucer	**farfurioară** (f)	[farfurio'arə]
glass (tumbler)	**pahar** (n)	[pa'har]
wine glass	**cupă** (f)	['kupə]
stock pot (soup pot)	**cratiţă** (f)	['kratit͡sə]
bottle (~ of wine)	**sticlă** (f)	['stiklə]
neck (of the bottle, etc.)	**gâtul** (n) **sticlei**	['gɨtul 'stiklej]
carafe (decanter)	**garafă** (f)	[ga'rafə]
pitcher	**ulcior** (n)	[ul't͡ʃior]
vessel (container)	**vas** (n)	[vas]
pot (crock, stoneware ~)	**oală** (f)	[o'alə]
vase	**vază** (f)	['vazə]
flacon, bottle (perfume ~)	**flacon** (n)	[fla'kon]
vial, small bottle	**sticluţă** (f)	[sti'klut͡sə]
tube (of toothpaste)	**tub** (n)	[tub]
sack (bag)	**sac** (m)	[sak]
bag (paper ~, plastic ~)	**pachet** (n)	[pa'ket]
pack (of cigarettes, etc.)	**pachet** (n)	[pa'ket]
box (e.g., shoebox)	**cutie** (f)	[ku'tie]
crate	**ladă** (f)	['ladə]
basket	**coş** (n)	[koʃ]

MAIN VERBS

T&P Books Publishing

to advise (vt)	a sfătui	[a sfətu'i]
to agree (say yes)	a fi de acord	[a fi de a'kord]
to answer (vi, vt)	a răspunde	[a rəs'punde]
to apologize (vi)	a cere scuze	[a 'ʧere 'skuze]
to arrive (vi)	a sosi	[a so'si]

to ask (~ oneself)	a întreba	[a intre'ba]
to ask (~ sb to do sth)	a cere	[a 'ʧere]
to be (vi)	a fi	[a fi]

to be afraid	a se teme	[a se 'teme]
to be hungry	a fi foame	[a fi fo'ame]
to be interested in ...	a se interesa	[a se intere'sa]
to be needed	a fi necesar	[a fi neʧe'sar]
to be surprised	a se mira	[a se mi'ra]

to be thirsty	a fi sete	[a fi 'sete]
to begin (vt)	a începe	[a in'ʧepe]
to belong to ...	a aparține	[a apar'tsine]

| to boast (vi) | a se lăuda | [a se ləu'da] |
| to break (split into pieces) | a rupe | [a 'rupe] |

to call (~ for help)	a chema	[a ke'ma]
can (v aux)	a putea	[a pu'tʲa]
to catch (vt)	a prinde	[a 'prinde]

| to change (vt) | a schimba | [a skim'ba] |
| to choose (select) | a alege | [a a'ledʒe] |

to come down (the stairs)	a coborî	[a kobo'ri]
to compare (vt)	a compara	[a kompa'ra]
to complain (vi, vt)	a se plânge	[a se 'plindʒe]
to confuse (mix up)	a încurca	[a inkur'ka]

| to continue (vt) | a continua | [a kontinu'a] |
| to control (vt) | a controla | [a kontro'la] |

to cook (dinner)	a găti	[a gə'ti]
to cost (vt)	a costa	[a kos'ta]
to count (add up)	a calcula	[a kalku'la]
to count on ...	a conta pe ...	[a kon'ta pe]
to create (vt)	a crea	[a 'krʲa]
to cry (weep)	a plânge	[a 'plindʒe]

14. The most important verbs. Part 2

to deceive (vi, vt)	a minți	[a min'tsi]
to decorate (tree, street)	a împodobi	[a impodo'bi]
to defend (a country, etc.)	a apăra	[a ape'ra]
to demand (request firmly)	a cere	[a 'tfere]
to dig (vt)	a săpa	[a sə'pa]
to discuss (vt)	a discuta	[a disku'ta]
to do (vt)	a face	[a 'fatfe]
to doubt (have doubts)	a se îndoi	[a se indo'i]
to drop (let fall)	a scăpa	[a skə'pa]
to enter	a intra	[a in'tra]
(room, house, etc.)		
to excuse (forgive)	a scuza	[a sku'za]
to exist (vi)	a exista	[a ekzis'ta]
to expect (foresee)	a prevedea	[a preve'dʲa]
to explain (vt)	a explica	[a ekspli'ka]
to fall (vi)	a cădea	[a kə'dʲa]
to find (vt)	a găsi	[a gə'si]
to finish (vt)	a termina	[a termi'na]
to fly (vi)	a zbura	[a zbu'ra]
to follow ... (come after)	a urma	[a ur'ma]
to forget (vi, vt)	a uita	[a uj'ta]
to forgive (vt)	a ierta	[a er'ta]
to give (vt)	a da	[a da]
to give a hint	a face aluzie	[a 'fatfe a'luzie]
to go (on foot)	a merge	[a 'merdʒe]
to go for a swim	a se scălda	[a se skəl'da]
to go out (for dinner, etc.)	a ieşi	[a e'ʃi]
to guess (the answer)	a ghici	[a gi'tʃi]
to have (vt)	a avea	[a a'vʲa]
to have breakfast	a lua micul dejun	[a lu'a 'mikul de'ʒun]
to have dinner	a cina	[a tʃi'na]
to have lunch	a lua prânzul	[a lu'a 'prinzul]
to hear (vt)	a auzi	[a au'zi]
to help (vt)	a ajuta	[a aʒu'ta]
to hide (vt)	a ascunde	[a as'kunde]
to hope (vi, vt)	a spera	[a spe'ra]
to hunt (vi, vt)	a vâna	[a vi'na]
to hurry (vi)	a se grăbi	[a se grə'bi]

15. The most important verbs. Part 3

to inform (vt)	a informa	[a infor'ma]
to insist (vi, vt)	a insista	[a insis'ta]
to insult (vt)	a jigni	[a ʒig'ni]
to invite (vt)	a invita	[a invi'ta]
to joke (vi)	a glumi	[a glu'mi]
to keep (vt)	a păstra	[a pəs'tra]
to keep silent, to hush	a tăcea	[a tə'tʃa]
to kill (vt)	a omorî	[a omo'rɨ]
to know (sb)	a cunoaşte	[a kuno'aʃte]
to know (sth)	a şti	[a ʃti]
to laugh (vi)	a râde	[a 'rɨde]
to liberate (city, etc.)	a elibera	[a elibe'ra]
to like (I like ...)	a plăcea	[a plə'tʃa]
to look for ... (search)	a căuta	[a kəu'ta]
to love (sb)	a iubi	[a ju'bi]
to make a mistake	a greşi	[a gre'ʃi]
to manage, to run	a conduce	[a kon'dutʃe]
to mean (signify)	a însemna	[a ɨnsem'na]
to mention (talk about)	a menţiona	[a mentsio'na]
to miss (school, etc.)	a lipsi	[a lip'si]
to notice (see)	a observa	[a obser'va]
to object (vi, vt)	a contrazice	[a kontra'zitʃe]
to observe (see)	a observa	[a obser'va]
to open (vt)	a deschide	[a des'kide]
to order (meal, etc.)	a comanda	[a koman'da]
to order (mil.)	a ordona	[a ordo'na]
to own (possess)	a poseda	[a pose'da]
to participate (vi)	a participa	[a partitʃi'pa]
to pay (vi, vt)	a plăti	[a plə'ti]
to permit (vt)	a permite	[a per'mite]
to plan (vt)	a planifica	[a planifi'ka]
to play (children)	a juca	[a ʒu'ka]
to pray (vi, vt)	a se ruga	[a se ru'ga]
to prefer (vt)	a prefera	[a prefe'ra]
to promise (vt)	a promite	[a pro'mite]
to pronounce (vt)	a pronunţa	[a pronun'tsa]
to propose (vt)	a propune	[a pro'pune]
to punish (vt)	a pedepsi	[a pedep'si]

16. The most important verbs. Part 4

to read (vi, vt)	a citi	[a tʃi'ti]
to recommend (vt)	a recomanda	[a rekoman'da]

to refuse (vi, vt)	a refuza	[a refu'za]
to regret (be sorry)	a regreta	[a regre'ta]
to rent (sth from sb)	a închiria	[a ɨnkiri'ja]
to repeat (say again)	a repeta	[a repe'ta]
to reserve, to book	a rezerva	[a rezer'va]
to run (vi)	a alerga	[a aler'ga]
to save (rescue)	a salva	[a sal'va]
to say (~ thank you)	a spune	[a 'spune]
to scold (vt)	a certa	[a tʃer'ta]
to see (vt)	a vedea	[a ve'dʲa]
to sell (vt)	a vinde	[a 'vinde]
to send (vt)	a trimite	[a tri'mite]
to shoot (vi)	a trage	[a 'tradʒe]
to shout (vi)	a striga	[a stri'ga]
to show (vt)	a arăta	[a arə'ta]
to sign (document)	a semna	[a sem'na]
to sit down (vi)	a se aşeza	[a se aʃə'za]
to smile (vi)	a zâmbi	[a zɨm'bi]
to speak (vi, vt)	a vorbi	[a vor'bi]
to steal (money, etc.)	a fura	[a fu'ra]
to stop (for pause, etc.)	a se opri	[a se o'pri]
to stop (please ~ calling me)	a înceta	[a antʃe'ta]
to study (vt)	a studia	[a studi'a]
to swim (vi)	a înota	[a ɨno'ta]
to take (vt)	a lua	[a lu'a]
to think (vi, vt)	a se gândi	[a se gɨn'di]
to threaten (vt)	a ameninţa	[a amenin'tsa]
to touch (with hands)	a atinge	[a a'tindʒe]
to translate (vt)	a traduce	[a tra'dutʃe]
to trust (vt)	a avea încredere	[a a'vʲa ɨn'kredere]
to try (attempt)	a încerca	[a ɨntʃer'ka]
to turn (e.g., ~ left)	a întoarce	[a ɨnto'artʃe]
to underestimate (vt)	a subaprecia	[a subapretʃi'a]
to understand (vt)	a înţelege	[a ɨntse'ledʒe]
to unite (vt)	a uni	[a u'ni]
to wait (vt)	a aştepta	[a aʃtep'ta]
to want (wish, desire)	a vrea	[a vrʲa]
to warn (vt)	a avertiza	[a averti'za]
to work (vi)	a lucra	[a lu'kra]
to write (vt)	a scrie	[a 'skrie]
to write down	a nota	[a no'ta]

TIME. CALENDAR

T&P Books Publishing

Monday	luni (f)	[lunʲ]
Tuesday	marți (f)	['martsʲ]
Wednesday	miercuri (f)	['merkurʲ]
Thursday	joi (f)	[ʒoj]
Friday	vineri (f)	['vinerʲ]
Saturday	sâmbătă (f)	['sɨmbətə]
Sunday	duminică (f)	[du'minikə]

today (adv)	astăzi	['astəzʲ]
tomorrow (adv)	mâine	['mɨjne]
the day after tomorrow	poimâine	[poj'mɨne]
yesterday (adv)	ieri	[jerʲ]
the day before yesterday	alaltăieri	[a'laltəerʲ]

day	zi (f)	[zi]
working day	zi (f) de lucru	[zi de 'lukru]
public holiday	zi (f) de sărbătoare	[zi de sərbəto'are]
day off	zi (f) liberă	[zi 'liberə]
weekend	zile (f pl) de odihnă	['zile de o'dihnə]

all day long	toată ziua	[to'atə 'ziwa]
the next day (adv)	a doua zi	['dowa zi]
two days ago	cu două zile în urmă	[ku 'dowə 'zile ɨn 'urmə]
the day before	în ajun	[ɨn a'ʒun]
daily (adj)	zilnic	['zilnik]
every day (adv)	în fiecare zi	[ɨn fie'kare zi]

week	săptămână (f)	[səptə'mɨnə]
last week (adv)	săptămâna trecută	[səptə'mɨna tre'kutə]
next week (adv)	săptămâna viitoare	[səptə'mɨna viito'are]
weekly (adj)	săptămânal	[səptəmɨ'nal]
every week (adv)	în fiecare săptămână	[ɨn fie'kare səptə'mɨnə]
twice a week	de două ori pe săptămână	[de 'dowə orʲ pe səptə'mɨnə]
every Tuesday	în fiecare marți	[ɨn fie'kare 'martsʲ]

morning	dimineață (f)	[dimi'nʲatsə]
in the morning	dimineața	[dimi'nʲatsa]
noon, midday	amiază (f)	[a'mjazə]
in the afternoon	după masă	['dupə 'masə]

evening	seară (f)	['sʲarə]
in the evening	seara	['sʲara]
night	noapte (f)	[no'apte]
at night	noaptea	[no'aptʲa]
midnight	miezul (n) nopţii	['mezul 'noptsij]

second	secundă (f)	[se'kundə]
minute	minut (n)	[mi'nut]
hour	oră (f)	['orə]
half an hour	jumătate de oră	[ʒumə'tate de 'orə]
a quarter-hour	un sfert de oră	[un sfert de 'orə]
fifteen minutes	cincisprezece minute	['tʃintʃsprezetʃe mi'nute]
24 hours	o zi (f)	[o zi]

sunrise	răsărit (n)	[rəsə'rit]
dawn	zori (m pl)	[zorʲ]
early morning	zori (m pl) de zi	[zorʲ de zi]
sunset	apus (n)	[a'pus]

early in the morning	dimineaţa devreme	[dimi'nʲatsa de'vreme]
this morning	azi dimineaţă	[azʲ dimi'nʲatsə]
tomorrow morning	mâine dimineaţă	['mɨjne dimi'nʲatsə]

this afternoon	această după-amiază	[a'tʃastə 'dupa ami'azə]
in the afternoon	după masă	['dupə 'masə]
tomorrow afternoon	mâine după-masă	['mɨjne 'dupə 'masə]

| tonight (this evening) | astă-seară | ['astə 'sʲarə] |
| tomorrow night | mâine seară | ['mɨjne 'sʲarə] |

at 3 o'clock sharp	la ora trei fix	[la 'ora trej fiks]
about 4 o'clock	în jur de ora patru	[ɨn ʒur de 'ora 'patru]
by 12 o'clock	pe la ora douăsprezece	[pe la 'ora 'dowəsprezetʃe]

in 20 minutes	peste douăzeci de minute	['peste dowə'zetʃi de mi'nute]
in an hour	peste o oră	['peste o 'orə]
on time (adv)	la timp	[la timp]

a quarter to …	fără un sfert	['fərə un sfert]
within an hour	în decurs de o oră	[ɨn de'kurs de o 'orə]
every 15 minutes	la fiecare cincisprezece minute	[la fie'kare 'tʃintʃsprezetʃe mi'nute]
round the clock	zi şi noapte	[zi ʃi no'apte]

19. Months. Seasons

January	ianuarie (m)	[janu'arie]
February	februarie (m)	[febru'arie]
March	martie (m)	['martie]

April	aprilie (m)	[a'prilie]
May	mai (m)	[maj]
June	iunie (m)	['junie]

July	iulie (m)	['julie]
August	august (m)	['august]
September	septembrie (m)	[sep'tembrie]
October	octombrie (m)	[ok'tombrie]
November	noiembrie (m)	[no'embrie]
December	decembrie (m)	[de'tʃembrie]

spring	primăvară (f)	[primə'varə]
in spring	primăvara	[primə'vara]
spring (as adj)	de primăvară	[de primə'varə]

summer	vară (f)	['varə]
in summer	vara	['vara]
summer (as adj)	de vară	[de 'varə]

fall	toamnă (f)	[to'amnə]
in fall	toamna	[to'amna]
fall (as adj)	de toamnă	[de to'amnə]

winter	iarnă (f)	['jarnə]
in winter	iarna	['jarna]
winter (as adj)	de iarnă	[de 'jarnə]

month	lună (f)	['lunə]
this month	în luna curentă	[ɨn 'luna ku'rentə]
next month	în luna următoare	[ɨn 'luna urməto'are]
last month	în luna trecută	[ɨn 'luna tre'kutə]

a month ago	o lună în urmă	[o 'lunə ɨn 'urmə]
in a month (a month later)	peste o lună	['peste o 'lunə]
in 2 months (2 months later)	peste două luni	['peste 'dowə lunʲ]
the whole month	luna întreagă	['luna ɨn'trʲagə]
all month long	o lună întreagă	[o 'lunə ɨn'trʲagə]

monthly (~ magazine)	lunar	[lu'nar]
monthly (adv)	în fiecare lună	[ɨn fie'kare 'lunə]
every month	fiecare lună	[fie'kare 'lunə]
twice a month	de două ori pe lună	[de 'dowə orʲ pe 'lunə]

year	an (m)	[an]
this year	anul acesta	['anul a'tʃesta]
next year	anul viitor	['anul vii'tor]
last year	anul trecut	['anul tre'kut]

a year ago	acum un an	[a'kum un an]
in a year	peste un an	['peste un an]
in two years	peste doi ani	['peste doj anʲ]

the whole year	tot anul	[tot 'anul]
all year long	un an întreg	[un an ɨn'treg]
every year	în fiecare an	[ɨn fie'kare an]
annual (adj)	anual	[anu'al]
annually (adv)	în fiecare an	[ɨn fie'kare an]
4 times a year	de patru ori pe an	[de 'patru orⁱ pe an]
date (e.g., today's ~)	dată (f)	['datə]
date (e.g., ~ of birth)	dată (f)	['datə]
calendar	calendar (n)	[kalen'dar]
half a year	jumătate (f) de an	[ʒumə'tate de an]
six months	jumătate (f) de an	[ʒumə'tate de an]
season (summer, etc.)	sezon (n)	[se'zon]
century	veac (n)	[vⁱak]

TRAVEL. HOTEL

T&P Books Publishing

20. Trip. Travel

tourism, travel	**turism** (n)	[tu'rism]
tourist	**turist** (m)	[tu'rist]
trip, voyage	**călătorie** (f)	[kələto'rie]
adventure	**aventură** (f)	[aven'turə]
trip, journey	**voiaj** (n)	[vo'jaʒ]
vacation	**concediu** (n)	[kon'tʃedju]
to be on vacation	**a fi în concediu**	[a fi ɨn kon'tʃedju]
rest	**odihnă** (f)	[o'dihnə]
train	**tren** (n)	[tren]
by train	**cu trenul**	[ku 'trenul]
airplane	**avion** (n)	[a'vjon]
by airplane	**cu avionul**	[ku a'vjonul]
by car	**cu automobilul**	[ku automo'bilul]
by ship	**cu vaporul**	[ku va'porul]
luggage	**bagaj** (n)	[ba'gaʒ]
suitcase	**valiză** (f)	[va'lizə]
luggage cart	**cărucior** (n) **pentru bagaj**	[kəru'tʃior 'pentru ba'gaʒ]
passport	**paşaport** (n)	[paʃa'port]
visa	**viză** (f)	['vizə]
ticket	**bilet** (n)	[bi'let]
air ticket	**bilet** (n) **de avion**	[bi'let de a'vjon]
guidebook	**ghid** (m)	[gid]
map (tourist ~)	**hartă** (f)	['hartə]
area (rural ~)	**localitate** (f)	[lokali'tate]
place, site	**loc** (n)	[lok]
exotica (n)	**exotism** (n)	[egzo'tism]
exotic (adj)	**exotic**	[e'gzotik]
amazing (adj)	**uimitor**	[ujmi'tor]
group	**grup** (n)	[grup]
excursion, sightseeing tour	**excursie** (f)	[eks'kursie]
guide (person)	**ghid** (m)	[gid]

21. Hotel

hotel	**hotel** (n)	[ho'tel]
motel	**motel** (n)	[mo'tel]

three-star (~ hotel)	**trei stele**	[trej 'stele]
five-star	**cinci stele**	[tʃintʃ 'stele]
to stay (in a hotel, etc.)	**a se opri**	[a se o'pri]
room	**cameră** (f)	['kamerə]
single room	**cameră pentru o persoană** (n)	['kamerə 'pentru o perso'anə]
double room	**cameră pentru două persoane** (n)	['kamerə 'pentru 'dowə perso'ane]
to book a room	**a rezerva o cameră**	[a rezer'va o 'kamerə]
half board	**demipensiune** (f)	[demipensi'une]
full board	**pensiune** (f)	[pensi'une]
with bath	**cu baie**	[ku 'bae]
with shower	**cu duş**	[ku duʃ]
satellite television	**televiziune** (f) **prin satelit**	[televizi'une 'prin sate'lit]
air-conditioner	**aer** (n) **condiţionat**	['aer konditsio'nat]
towel	**prosop** (n)	[pro'sop]
key	**cheie** (f)	['kee]
administrator	**administrator** (m)	[adminis'trator]
chambermaid	**femeie** (f) **de serviciu**	[fe'mee de ser'vitʃiu]
porter, bellboy	**hamal** (m)	[ha'mal]
doorman	**portar** (m)	[por'tar]
restaurant	**restaurant** (n)	[restau'rant]
pub, bar	**bar** (n)	[bar]
breakfast	**micul dejun** (n)	['mikul de'ʒun]
dinner	**cină** (f)	['tʃinə]
buffet	**masă suedeză** (f)	['masə sue'dezə]
lobby	**vestibul** (n)	[vesti'bul]
elevator	**lift** (n)	[lift]
DO NOT DISTURB	**NU DERANJAŢI!**	[nu deran'ʒats]
NO SMOKING	**NU FUMAŢI!**	[nu fu'mats]

22. Sightseeing

monument	**monument** (n)	[monu'ment]
fortress	**cetate** (f)	[tʃe'tate]
palace	**palat** (n)	[pa'lat]
castle	**castel** (n)	[kas'tel]
tower	**turn** (n)	[turn]
mausoleum	**mausoleu** (n)	[mawzo'leu]
architecture	**arhitectură** (f)	[arhitek'turə]
medieval (adj)	**medieval**	[medie'val]
ancient (adj)	**vechi**	[vekʲ]

| national (adj) | național | [natsio'nal] |
| famous (monument, etc.) | cunoscut | [kunos'kut] |

tourist	turist (m)	[tu'rist]
guide (person)	ghid (m)	[gid]
excursion, sightseeing tour	excursie (f)	[eks'kursie]
to show (vt)	a arăta	[a arə'ta]
to tell (vt)	a povesti	[a poves'ti]

to find (vt)	a găsi	[a gə'si]
to get lost (lose one's way)	a se pierde	[a se 'pjerde]
map (e.g., subway ~)	schemă (f)	['skemə]
map (e.g., city ~)	plan (m)	[plan]

| souvenir, gift | suvenir (n) | [suve'nir] |
| gift shop | magazin (n) de suveniruri | [maga'zin de suve'niruri] |

| to take pictures | a fotografia | [a fotografi'ja] |
| to have one's picture taken | a se fotografia | [a se fotografi'ja] |

TRANSPORTATION

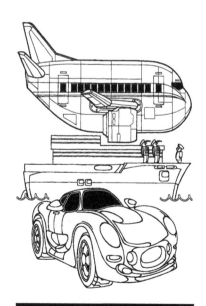

T&P Books Publishing

23. Airport

airport	**aeroport** (n)	[aero'port]
airplane	**avion** (n)	[a'vjon]
airline	**companie** (f) **aeriană**	[kompa'nie aeri'anə]
air traffic controller	**dispecer** (n)	[dis'petʃer]
departure	**decolare** (f)	[deko'lare]
arrival	**aterizare** (f)	[ateri'zare]
to arrive (by plane)	**a ateriza**	[a ateri'za]
departure time	**ora** (f) **decolării**	['ora dekolərij]
arrival time	**ora** (f) **aterizării**	['ora aterizərij]
to be delayed	**a întârzia**	[a ɨntɨr'zija]
flight delay	**întârzierea** (f) **zborului**	[ɨntɨrzjer'a 'zboruluj]
information board	**panou** (n)	[pa'nou]
information	**informație** (f)	[infor'matsie]
to announce (vt)	**a anunța**	[a anun'tsa]
flight (e.g., next ~)	**cursă** (f)	['kursə]
customs	**vamă** (f)	['vamə]
customs officer	**vameş** (m)	['vameʃ]
customs declaration	**declarație** (f)	[dekla'ratsie]
to fill out (vt)	**a completa**	[a komple'ta]
to fill out the declaration	**a completa declarația**	[a komple'ta dekla'ratsija]
passport control	**controlul** (n) **paşapoartelor**	[kon'trolul paʃapo'artelor]
luggage	**bagaj** (n)	[ba'gaʒ]
hand luggage	**bagaj** (n) **de mână**	[ba'gaʒ de 'mɨnə]
luggage cart	**cărucior** (n) **pentru bagaj**	[kəru'tʃior 'pentru ba'gaʒ]
landing	**aterizare** (f)	[ateri'zare]
landing strip	**pistă** (f) **de aterizare**	['pistə de ateri'zare]
to land (vi)	**a ateriza**	[a ateri'za]
airstair (passenger stair)	**scară** (f)	['skarə]
check-in	**înregistrare** (f)	[ɨnredʒis'trare]
check-in counter	**birou** (n) **de înregistrare**	[bi'rou de ɨnredʒis'trare]
to check-in (vi)	**a se înregistra**	[a se ɨnredʒis'tra]
boarding pass	**număr** (n) **de bord**	['numər de bord]
departure gate	**debarcare** (f)	[debar'kare]
transit	**tranzit** (n)	['tranzit]

to wait (vt)	a aştepta	[a aʃtep'ta]
departure lounge	sală (f) de aşteptare	['sale de aʃtep'tare]
to see off	a conduce	[a kon'dutʃe]
to say goodbye	a-şi lua rămas bun	[aʃ lu'a rə'mas bun]

24. Airplane

airplane	avion (n)	[a'vjon]
air ticket	bilet (n) de avion	[bi'let de a'vjon]
airline	companie (f) aeriană	[kompa'nie aeri'ane]
airport	aeroport (n)	[aero'port]
supersonic (adj)	supersonic	[super'sonik]

captain	comandant (m) de navă	[koman'dant de 'nave]
crew	echipaj (n)	[eki'paʒ]
pilot	pilot (m)	[pi'lot]
flight attendant (fem.)	stewardesă (f)	[stjuar'dese]
navigator	navigator (m)	[naviga'tor]

wings	aripi (f pl)	[a'ripʲ]
tail	coadă (f)	[ko'ade]
cockpit	cabină (f)	[ka'bine]
engine	motor (n)	[mo'tor]
undercarriage (landing gear)	tren (n) de aterizare	[tren de ateri'zare]
turbine	turbină (f)	[tur'bine]

propeller	elice (f)	[e'litʃe]
black box	cutie (f) neagră	[ku'tie 'nʲagre]
yoke (control column)	manşă (f)	['manʃe]
fuel	combustibil (m)	[kombus'tibil]

safety card	instrucţiune (f)	[instruktsi'une]
oxygen mask	mască (f) cu oxigen	['maske 'ku oksi'dʒen]
uniform	uniformă (f)	[uni'forme]
life vest	vestă (f) de salvare	['veste de sal'vare]
parachute	paraşută (f)	[para'ʃute]

takeoff	decolare (f)	[deko'lare]
to take off (vi)	a decola	[a deko'la]
runway	pistă (f) de decolare	['piste de deko'lare]

visibility	vizibilitate (f)	[vizibili'tate]
flight (act of flying)	zbor (n)	[zbor]
altitude	înălţime (f)	[inəl'tsime]
air pocket	gol de aer (n)	[gol de 'aer]

seat	loc (n)	[lok]
headphones	căşti (f pl)	[kəʃtʲ]
folding tray (tray table)	măsuţă (f) rabatabilă	[mə'sutsə raba'tabile]

airplane window	**hublou** (n)	[hu'blou]
aisle	**trecere** (f)	['tretʃere]

25. Train

train	**tren** (n)	[tren]
commuter train	**tren** (n) **electric**	['tren e'lektrik]
express train	**tren** (n) **accelerat**	['tren aktʃele'rat]
diesel locomotive	**locomotivă** (f) **cu motor diesel**	[lokomo'tivə ku mo'tor 'dizel]
steam locomotive	**locomotivă** (f)	[lokomo'tivə]
passenger car	**vagon** (n)	[va'gon]
dining car	**vagon-restaurant** (n)	[va'gon restau'rant]
rails	**şine** (f pl)	['ʃine]
railroad	**cale** (f) **ferată**	['kale fe'ratə]
railway tie	**traversă** (f)	[tra'versə]
platform (railway ~)	**peron** (n)	[pe'ron]
track (~ 1, 2, etc.)	**linie** (f)	['linie]
semaphore	**semafor** (n)	[sema'for]
station	**staţie** (f)	['statsie]
engineer (train driver)	**maşinist** (m)	[maʃi'nist]
porter (of luggage)	**hamal** (m)	[ha'mal]
car attendant	**însoţitor** (m)	[ɨnsotsi'tor]
passenger	**pasager** (m)	[pasa'dʒer]
conductor (ticket inspector)	**controlor** (m)	[kontro'lor]
corridor (in train)	**coridor** (n)	[kori'dor]
emergency brake	**semnal** (n) **de alarmă**	[sem'nal de a'larmə]
compartment	**compartiment** (n)	[komparti'ment]
berth	**cuşetă** (f)	[ku'ʃetə]
upper berth	**patul** (n) **de sus**	['patul de sus]
lower berth	**patul** (n) **de jos**	['patul de ʒos]
bed linen, bedding	**lenjerie** (f) **de pat**	[lenʒe'rie de pat]
ticket	**bilet** (n)	[bi'let]
schedule	**orar** (n)	[o'rar]
information display	**panou** (n)	[pa'nou]
to leave, to depart	**a pleca**	[a ple'ka]
departure (of train)	**plecare** (f)	[ple'kare]
to arrive (ab. train)	**a sosi**	[a so'si]
arrival	**sosire** (f)	[so'sire]
to arrive by train	**a veni cu trenul**	[a ve'ni ku 'trenul]
to get on the train	**a se aşeza în tren**	[a se aʃe'za ɨn tren]

to get off the train	a coborî din tren	[a kobo'rɨ din tren]
train wreck	accident (n) de tren	[aktʃi'dent de tren]
to derail (vi)	a deraia	[dera'ja]
steam locomotive	locomotivă (f)	[lokomo'tivə]
stoker, fireman	fochist (m)	[fo'kist]
firebox	focar (n)	[fo'kar]
coal	cărbune (m)	[kər'bune]

26. Ship

ship	corabie (f)	[ko'rabie]
vessel	navă (f)	['navə]
steamship	vapor (n)	[va'por]
riverboat	motonavă (f)	[moto'navə]
cruise ship	vas (n) de croazieră	[vas de kroa'zjerə]
cruiser	crucişător (n)	[krutʃiʃə'tor]
yacht	iaht (n)	[jaht]
tugboat	remorcher (n)	[remor'ker]
barge	şlep (n)	[ʃlep]
ferry	bac (n)	[bak]
sailing ship	velier (n)	[ve'ljer]
brigantine	brigantină (f)	[brigan'tinə]
ice breaker	spărgător (n) de gheaţă	[spərgə'tor de 'gʲatsə]
submarine	submarin (n)	[subma'rin]
boat (flat-bottomed ~)	barcă (f)	['barkə]
dinghy	şalupă (f)	[ʃa'lupə]
lifeboat	şalupă (f) de salvare	[ʃa'lupə de sal'vare]
motorboat	cuter (n)	['kuter]
captain	căpitan (m)	[kəpi'tan]
seaman	marinar (m)	[mari'nar]
sailor	marinar (m)	[mari'nar]
crew	echipaj (n)	[eki'paʒ]
boatswain	şef (m) de echipaj	[ʃef de eki'paʒ]
ship's boy	mus (m)	[mus]
cook	bucătar (m)	[buke'tar]
ship's doctor	medic (m) pe navă	['medik pe 'navə]
deck	teugă (f)	[te'ugə]
mast	catarg (n)	[ka'targ]
sail	velă (f)	['velə]
hold	cală (f)	['kalə]
bow (prow)	proră (f)	['prorə]

stern	**pupă** (f)	['pupə]
oar	**vâslă** (f)	['vɨslə]
screw propeller	**elice** (f)	[e'litʃe]
cabin	**cabină** (f)	[ka'binə]
wardroom	**salonul** (n) **ofițerilor**	[sa'lonul ofi'tserilor]
engine room	**sala** (f) **mașinilor**	['sala ma'ʃinilor]
bridge	**punte** (f) **de comandă**	['punte de ko'mandə]
radio room	**stație** (f) **de radio**	['statsie de 'radio]
wave (radio)	**undă** (f)	['undə]
logbook	**jurnal** (n) **de bord**	[ʒur'nal de bord]
spyglass	**lunetă** (f)	[lu'netə]
bell	**clopot** (n)	['klopot]
flag	**steag** (n)	['stʲag]
hawser (mooring ~)	**parâmă** (f)	[pa'rɨmə]
knot (bowline, etc.)	**nod** (n)	[nod]
deckrails	**bară** (f)	['barə]
gangway	**pasarelă** (f)	[pasa'relə]
anchor	**ancoră** (f)	['ankorə]
to weigh anchor	**a ridica ancora**	[a ridi'ka 'ankora]
to drop anchor	**a ancora**	[a anko'ra]
anchor chain	**lanț** (n) **de ancoră**	[lants de 'ankorə]
port (harbor)	**port** (n)	[port]
quay, wharf	**acostare** (f)	[akos'tare]
to berth (moor)	**a acosta**	[a akos'ta]
to cast off	**a demara**	[a dema'ra]
trip, voyage	**călătorie** (f)	[kələto'rie]
cruise (sea trip)	**croazieră** (f)	[kroa'zjerə]
course (route)	**direcție** (f)	[di'rektsie]
route (itinerary)	**rută** (f)	['rutə]
fairway	**cale** (f) **navigabilă**	['kale navi'gabilə]
(safe water channel)		
shallows	**banc** (n) **de nisip**	[bank de ni'sip]
to run aground	**a se împotmoli**	[a se ɨmpotmo'li]
storm	**furtună** (f)	[fur'tunə]
signal	**semnal** (n)	[sem'nal]
to sink (vi)	**a se scufunda**	[a se skufun'da]
Man overboard!	**Om la apă!**	[om la 'apə]
SOS (distress signal)	**SOS**	[sos]
ring buoy	**colac** (m) **de salvare**	[ko'lak de sal'vare]

CITY

T&P Books Publishing

bus	autobuz (n)	[auto'buz]
streetcar	tramvai (n)	[tram'vaj]
trolley bus	troleibuz (n)	[trolej'buz]
route (of bus, etc.)	rută (f)	['rutə]
number (e.g., bus ~)	număr (n)	['numər]
to go by ...	a merge cu ...	[a 'merʤe ku]
to get on (~ the bus)	a se urca	[a se ur'ka]
to get off ...	a coborî	[a kobo'rɨ]
stop (e.g., bus ~)	stație (f)	['staʦie]
next stop	stația (f) următoare	['staʦija urməto'are]
terminus	ultima stație (f)	['ultima 'staʦie]
schedule	orar (n)	[o'rar]
to wait (vt)	a aştepta	[a aʃtep'ta]
ticket	bilet (n)	[bi'let]
fare	costul (n) biletului	['kostul bi'letuluj]
cashier (ticket seller)	casier (m)	[ka'sjer]
ticket inspection	control (n)	[kon'trol]
ticket inspector	controlor (m)	[kontro'lor]
to be late (for ...)	a întârzia	[a ɨntɨr'zija]
to miss (~ the train, etc.)	a pierde ...	[a 'pjerdə]
to be in a hurry	a se grăbi	[a se grə'bi]
taxi, cab	taxi (n)	[ta'ksi]
taxi driver	taximetrist (m)	[taksime'trist]
by taxi	cu taxiul	[ku ta'ksjul]
taxi stand	stație (f) de taxiuri	['staʦie de ta'ksjurʲ]
to call a taxi	a chema un taxi	[a ke'ma un ta'ksi]
to take a taxi	a lua un taxi	[a lu'a un ta'ksi]
traffic	circulație (f) pe stradă	[ʧirku'laʦie pe 'stradə]
traffic jam	ambuteiaj (n)	[ambute'jaʒ]
rush hour	oră (f) de vârf	[orə de vɨrf]
to park (vi)	a se parca	[a se par'ka]
to park (vt)	a parca	[a par'ka]
parking lot	parcare (f)	[par'kare]
subway	metrou (n)	[me'trou]
station	stație (f)	['staʦie]
to take the subway	a merge cu metroul	[a 'merʤe ku me'troul]

| train | **tren** (n) | [tren] |
| train station | **gară** (f) | ['garə] |

28. City. Life in the city

city, town	**oraş** (n)	[o'raʃ]
capital city	**capitală** (f)	[kapi'talə]
village	**sat** (n)	[sat]

city map	**planul** (n) **oraşului**	['planul o'raʃuluj]
downtown	**centrul** (n) **oraşului**	['tʃentrul o'raʃuluj]
suburb	**suburbie** (f)	[subur'bie]
suburban (adj)	**din suburbie**	[din subur'bie]

outskirts	**margine** (f)	['mardʒine]
environs (suburbs)	**împrejurimi** (f pl)	[împreʒu'rimʲ]
city block	**cartier** (n)	[kar'tjer]
residential block (area)	**cartier** (n) **locativ**	[ka'rtjer loka'tiv]

traffic	**circulaţie** (f)	[tʃirku'latsie]
traffic lights	**semafor** (n)	[sema'for]
public transportation	**transport** (n) **urban**	[trans'port ur'ban]
intersection	**intersecţie** (f)	[inter'sektsie]

crosswalk	**trecere** (f)	['tretʃere]
pedestrian underpass	**trecere** (f) **subterană**	['tretʃere subte'ranə]
to cross (~ the street)	**a traversa**	[a traver'sa]
pedestrian	**pieton** (m)	[pie'ton]
sidewalk	**trotuar** (n)	[trotu'ar]

bridge	**pod** (n)	[pod]
embankment (river walk)	**faleză** (f)	[fa'lezə]
fountain	**havuz** (n)	[ha'vuz]

allée (garden walkway)	**alee** (f)	[a'lee]
park	**parc** (n)	[park]
boulevard	**bulevard** (n)	[bule'vard]
square	**piaţă** (f)	['pjatsə]
avenue (wide street)	**prospect** (n)	[pros'pekt]
street	**stradă** (f)	['stradə]
side street	**stradelă** (f)	[stra'delə]
dead end	**fundătură** (f)	[fundə'turə]

house	**casă** (f)	['kasə]
building	**clădire** (f)	[klə'dire]
skyscraper	**zgârie-nori** (m)	['zgîrie norʲ]

facade	**faţadă** (f)	[fa'tsadə]
roof	**acoperiş** (n)	[akope'riʃ]
window	**fereastră** (f)	[fe'rʲastrə]

arch	**arc** (n)	[ark]
column	**coloană** (f)	[kolo'anə]
corner	**colţ** (n)	[kolts]

store window	**vitrină** (f)	[vi'trinə]
signboard (store sign, etc.)	**firmă** (f)	['firmə]
poster (e.g., playbill)	**afiş** (n)	[a'fiʃ]
advertising poster	**afişaj** (n)	[afi'ʃaʒ]
billboard	**panou** (n) **publicitar**	[pa'nu publitʃi'tar]

garbage, trash	**gunoi** (n)	[gu'noj]
trash can (public ~)	**coş** (n) **de gunoi**	[koʃ de gu'noj]
to litter (vi)	**a face murdărie**	[a 'fatʃe murdə'rie]
garbage dump	**groapă** (f) **de gunoi**	[gro'apə de gu'noj]

phone booth	**cabină** (f) **telefonică**	[ka'binə tele'fonikə]
lamppost	**stâlp** (m) **de felinar**	[stɨlp de feli'nar]
bench (park ~)	**bancă** (f)	['bankə]

police officer	**poliţist** (m)	[poli'tsist]
police	**poliţie** (f)	[po'litsie]
beggar	**cerşetor** (m)	[tʃerʃe'tor]
homeless (n)	**vagabond** (m)	[vaga'bond]

29. Urban institutions

store	**magazin** (n)	[maga'zin]
drugstore, pharmacy	**farmacie** (f)	[farma'tʃie]
eyeglass store	**optică** (f)	['optikə]
shopping mall	**centru** (n) **comercial**	['tʃentru komertʃi'al]
supermarket	**supermarket** (n)	[super'market]

bakery	**brutărie** (f)	[brutə'rie]
baker	**brutar** (m)	[bru'tar]
pastry shop	**cofetărie** (f)	[kofetə'rie]
grocery store	**băcănie** (f)	[bəkə'nie]
butcher shop	**hală** (f) **de carne**	['halə de 'karne]

produce store	**magazin** (m) **de legume**	[maga'zin de le'gume]
market	**piaţă** (f)	['pjatsə]

coffee house	**cafenea** (f)	[kafe'nʲa]
restaurant	**restaurant** (n)	[restau'rant]
pub, bar	**berărie** (f)	[berə'rie]
pizzeria	**pizzerie** (f)	[pitse'rie]

hair salon	**frizerie** (f)	[frize'rie]
post office	**poştă** (f)	['poʃtə]
dry cleaners	**curăţătorie** (f) **chimică**	[kurətseto'rie 'kimikə]
photo studio	**atelier** (n) **foto**	[ate'ljer 'foto]

shoe store	magazin (n) de încălţăminte	[maga'zin de ɨnkəltsə'minte]
bookstore	librărie (f)	[librə'rie]
sporting goods store	magazin (n) sportiv	[maga'zin spor'tiv]
clothes repair shop	croitorie (f)	[kroito'rie]
formal wear rental	închiriere (f) de haine	[ɨnki'rjere de 'hajne]
video rental store	închiriere (f) de filme	[ɨnki'rjere de 'filme]
circus	circ (n)	[tʃirk]
zoo	grădină (f) zoologică	[grə'dinə zoo'lodʒikə]
movie theater	cinematograf (n)	[tʃinemato'graf]
museum	muzeu (n)	[mu'zeu]
library	bibliotecă (f)	[biblio'tekə]
theater	teatru (n)	[te'atru]
opera (opera house)	operă (f)	['operə]
nightclub	club (n) de noapte	['klub de no'apte]
casino	cazinou (n)	[kazi'nou]
mosque	moschee (f)	[mos'kee]
synagogue	sinagogă (f)	[sina'gogə]
cathedral	catedrală (f)	[kate'dralə]
temple	templu (n)	['templu]
church	biserică (f)	[bi'serikə]
college	institut (n)	[insti'tut]
university	universitate (f)	[universi'tate]
school	şcoală (f)	[ʃko'alə]
prefecture	prefectură (f)	[prefek'turə]
city hall	primărie (f)	[primə'rie]
hotel	hotel (n)	[ho'tel]
bank	bancă (f)	['bankə]
embassy	ambasadă (f)	[amba'sadə]
travel agency	agenţie (f) de turism	[adʒen'tsie de tu'rism]
information office	birou (n) de informaţii	[bi'rou de infor'matsij]
currency exchange	schimb (n) valutar	[skimb valu'tar]
subway	metrou (n)	[me'trou]
hospital	spital (n)	[spi'tal]
gas station	benzinărie (f)	[benzinə'rie]
parking lot	parcare (f)	[par'kare]

30. Signs

signboard (store sign, etc.)	firmă (f)	['firmə]
notice (door sign, etc.)	inscripţie (f)	[in'skriptsie]

poster	afiş (n)	[a'fiʃ]
direction sign	semn (n)	[semn]
arrow (sign)	indicator (n)	[indika'tor]

caution	avertisment (n)	[avertis'ment]
warning sign	avertisment (n)	[avertis'ment]
to warn (vt)	a avertiza	[a averti'za]

rest day (weekly ~)	zi (f) de odihnă	[zi de o'dihnə]
timetable (schedule)	orar (n)	[o'rar]
opening hours	ore (f pl) de lucru	['ore de 'lukru]

WELCOME!	BINE AŢI VENIT!	['bine 'atsʲ ve'nit]
ENTRANCE	INTRARE	[in'trare]
EXIT	IEŞIRE	[je'ʃire]

PUSH	ÎMPINGE	[im'pindʒe]
PULL	TRAGE	['tradʒe]
OPEN	DESCHIS	[des'kis]
CLOSED	ÎNCHIS	[in'kis]

| WOMEN | PENTRU FEMEI | ['pentru fe'mej] |
| MEN | PENTRU BĂRBAŢI | ['pentru bər'batsʲ] |

DISCOUNTS	REDUCERI	[re'dutʃerʲ]
SALE	LICHIDARE DE STOC	[liki'dare de stok]
NEW!	NOU	['nou]
FREE	GRATUIT	[gratu'it]

ATTENTION!	ATENŢIE!	[a'tentsie]
NO VACANCIES	NU SUNT LOCURI	[nu 'sunt 'lokurʲ]
RESERVED	REZERVAT	[rezer'vat]

| ADMINISTRATION | ADMINISTRAŢIE | [adminis'tratsie] |
| STAFF ONLY | NUMAI PENTRU ANGAJAŢI | ['numaj 'pentru anga'ʒatsʲ] |

BEWARE OF THE DOG!	CÂINE RĂU	['kine 'rəu]
NO SMOKING	NU FUMAŢI!	[nu fu'matsʲ]
DO NOT TOUCH!	NU ATINGEŢI!	[nu a'tindʒetsʲ]

DANGEROUS	PERICULOS	[periku'los]
DANGER	PERICOL	[pe'rikol]
HIGH VOLTAGE	TENSIUNE ÎNALTĂ	[tensi'une i'naltə]

| NO SWIMMING! | SCĂLDATUL INTERZIS! | [skəl'datul inter'zis] |
| OUT OF ORDER | NU FUNCŢIONEAZĂ | [nu funktsio'nʲazə] |

FLAMMABLE	INFLAMABIL	[infla'mabil]
FORBIDDEN	INTERZIS	[inter'zis]
NO TRESPASSING!	TRECEREA INTERZISĂ	['tretʃerʲa inter'zisə]
WET PAINT	PROASPĂT VOPSIT	[pro'aspət vop'sit]

31. Shopping

to buy (purchase)	a cumpăra	[a kumpə'ra]
purchase	cumpărătură (f)	[kumpərə'turə]
to go shopping	a face cumpărături	[a 'fatʃe kumpərə'turʲ]
shopping (n)	shopping (n)	['ʃoping]
to be open (ab. store)	a fi deschis	[a fi des'kis]
to be closed	a se închide	[a se in'kide]
footwear, shoes	încălțăminte (f)	[inkəltsə'minte]
clothes, clothing	haine (f pl)	['hajne]
cosmetics	cosmetică (f)	[kos'metikə]
food products	produse (n pl)	[pro'duse]
gift, present	cadou (n)	[ka'dou]
salesman	vânzător (m)	[vinzə'tor]
saleswoman	vânzătoare (f)	[vinzəto'are]
check out, cash desk	casă (f)	['kasə]
mirror	oglindă (f)	[og'lində]
counter (store ~)	tejghea (f)	[teʒ'gʲa]
fitting room	cabină (f) de probă	[ka'binə de 'probə]
to try on	a proba	[a pro'ba]
to fit (ab. dress, etc.)	a veni	[a ve'ni]
to like (I like …)	a plăcea	[a plə'tʃa]
price	preț (n)	[prets]
price tag	indicator (n) de prețuri	[indika'tor de 'pretsurʲ]
to cost (vt)	a costa	[a kos'ta]
How much?	Cât?	[kit]
discount	reducere (f)	[re'dutʃere]
inexpensive (adj)	ieftin	['jeftin]
cheap (adj)	ieftin	['jeftin]
expensive (adj)	scump	[skump]
It's expensive	E scump	[e skump]
rental (n)	închiriere (f)	[inkiri'ere]
to rent (~ a tuxedo)	a lua în chirie	[a lu'a in ki'rie]
credit (trade credit)	credit (n)	['kredit]
on credit (adv)	în credit	[in 'kredit]

CLOTHING & ACCESSORIES

T&P Books Publishing

clothes	îmbrăcăminte (f)	[imbrəkə'minte]
outerwear	haină (f)	['hajnə]
winter clothing	îmbrăcăminte (f) de iarnă	[imbrəkə'minte de 'jarnə]

coat (overcoat)	palton (n)	[pal'ton]
fur coat	şubă (f)	['ʃubə]
fur jacket	scurtă (f) îmblănită	['skurtə imblə'nitə]
down coat	scurtă (f) de puf	['skurtə de 'puf]

jacket (e.g., leather ~)	scurtă (f)	['skurtə]
raincoat (trenchcoat, etc.)	trenci (f)	[trentʃi]
waterproof (adj)	impermeabil (n)	[imperme'abil]

shirt (button shirt)	cămaşă (f)	[kə'maʃə]
pants	pantaloni (m pl)	[panta'lonʲ]
jeans	blugi (m pl)	[bludʒʲ]
suit jacket	sacou (n)	[sa'kou]
suit	costum (n)	[kos'tum]

dress (frock)	rochie (f)	['rokie]
skirt	fustă (f)	['fustə]
blouse	bluză (f)	['bluzə]
knitted jacket (cardigan, etc.)	jachetă (f) tricotată	[ʒa'ketə triko'tatə]

| jacket (of woman's suit) | jachetă (f) | [ʒa'ketə] |

T-shirt	tricou (n)	[tri'kou]
shorts (short trousers)	şorturi (n pl)	['ʃorturʲ]
tracksuit	costum (n) sportiv	[kos'tum spor'tiv]
bathrobe	halat (n)	[ha'lat]
pajamas	pijama (f)	[piʒa'ma]

| sweater | sveter (n) | ['sveter] |
| pullover | pulover (n) | [pu'lover] |

vest	vestă (f)	['vestə]
tailcoat	frac (n)	[frak]
tuxedo	smoching (n)	['smoking]
uniform	uniformă (f)	[uni'formə]
workwear	haină (f) de lucru	['hajnə de 'lukru]

| overalls | salopetă (f) | [salo'petə] |
| coat (e.g., doctor's smock) | halat (n) | [ha'lat] |

34. Clothing. Underwear

underwear	lenjerie (f) de corp	[lenʒe'rie de 'korp]
boxers, briefs	boxeri, chiloţi (m pl)	[bokser'], [ki'lots']
panties	chiloţi (m pl)	[ki'lots']
undershirt (A-shirt)	maiou (n)	[ma'jou]
socks	şosete (f pl)	[ʃo'sete]

nightdress	cămaşă (f) de noapte	[kə'maʃə de no'apte]
bra	sutien (n)	[su'tjen]
knee highs (knee-high socks)	ciorapi (m pl)	[tʃio'rap']

pantyhose	ciorapi pantalon (m pl)	[tʃio'rap' panta'lon]
stockings (thigh highs)	ciorapi (m pl)	[tʃio'rap']
bathing suit	costum (n) de baie	[kos'tum de 'bae]

35. Headwear

hat	căciulă (f)	[kə'tʃiulə]
fedora	pălărie (f)	[pələ'rie]
baseball cap	şapcă (f)	['ʃapkə]
flatcap	chipiu (n)	[ki'pju]

beret	beretă (f)	[be'retə]
hood	glugă (f)	['glugə]
panama hat	panama (f)	[pana'ma]
knit cap (knitted hat)	căciulă (f) împletită	[kə'tʃiulə imple'titə]

| headscarf | basma (f) | [bas'ma] |
| women's hat | pălărie (f) de damă | [pələ'rie de 'damə] |

hard hat	cască (f)	['kaskə]
garrison cap	bonetă (f)	[bo'netə]
helmet	coif (n)	[kojf]

| derby | pălărie (f) | [pələ'rie] |
| top hat | joben (n) | [ʒo'ben] |

36. Footwear

footwear	încălţăminte (f)	[inkəltsə'minte]
shoes (men's shoes)	ghete (f pl)	['gete]
shoes (women's shoes)	pantofi (m pl)	[pan'tof']

| boots (e.g., cowboy ~) | cizme (f pl) | ['ʧizme] |
| slippers | şlapi (m pl) | [ʃlapʲ] |

tennis shoes (e.g., Nike ~)	adidaşi (m pl)	[a'didaʃ]
sneakers	tenişi (m pl)	['teniʃ]
(e.g., Converse ~)		
sandals	sandale (f pl)	[san'dale]

cobbler (shoe repairer)	cizmar (m)	[ʧiz'mar]
heel	toc (n)	[tok]
pair (of shoes)	pereche (f)	[pe'reke]

shoestring	şiret (n)	[ʃi'ret]
to lace (vt)	a şnurui	[a ʃnuru'i]
shoehorn	lingură (f) pentru pantofi	['lingurə 'pentru pan'tofʲ]
shoe polish	cremă (f) de ghete	['kremə de 'gete]

37. Personal accessories

gloves	mănuşi (f pl)	[mə'nuʃ]
mittens	mănuşi (f pl) cu un singur deget	[mə'nuʃ ku un 'singur 'dedʒet]
scarf (muffler)	fular (m)	[fu'lar]

glasses (eyeglasses)	ochelari (m pl)	[oke'larʲ]
frame (eyeglass ~)	ramă (f)	['ramə]
umbrella	umbrelă (f)	[um'brelə]
walking stick	baston (n)	[bas'ton]

| hairbrush | perie (f) de păr | [pe'rie de pər] |
| fan | evantai (n) | [evan'taj] |

| tie (necktie) | cravată (f) | [kra'vatə] |
| bow tie | papion (n) | [papi'on] |

| suspenders | bretele (f pl) | [bre'tele] |
| handkerchief | batistă (f) | [ba'tistə] |

| comb | pieptene (m) | ['pjeptene] |
| barrette | agrafă (f) | [a'grafə] |

| hairpin | ac (n) de păr | [ak de pər] |
| buckle | cataramă (f) | [kata'ramə] |

| belt | cordon (n) | [kor'don] |
| shoulder strap | curea (f) | [ku'rʲa] |

bag (handbag)	geantă (f)	['dʒantə]
purse	poşetă (f)	[po'ʃetə]
backpack	rucsac (n)	[ruk'sak]

38. Clothing. Miscellaneous

fashion	modă (f)	['modə]
in vogue (adj)	la modă	[la 'modə]
fashion designer	modelier (n)	[mode'ljer]
collar	guler (n)	['guler]
pocket	buzunar (n)	[buzu'nar]
pocket (as adj)	de buzunar	[de buzu'nar]
sleeve	mânecă (f)	['minekə]
hanging loop	gaică (f)	['gajkə]
fly (on trousers)	şliţ (n)	[ʃlits]
zipper (fastener)	fermoar (n)	[fermo'ar]
fastener	capsă (f)	['kapsə]
button	nasture (m)	['nasture]
buttonhole	butonieră (f)	[buto'njerə]
to come off (ab. button)	a se rupe	[a se 'rupe]
to sew (vi, vt)	a coase	[a ko'ase]
to embroider (vi, vt)	a broda	[a bro'da]
embroidery	broderie (f)	[brode'rie]
sewing needle	ac (n)	[ak]
thread	aţă (f)	['atsə]
seam	cusătură (f)	[kusə'turə]
to get dirty (vi)	a se murdări	[a se murdə'ri]
stain (mark, spot)	pată (f)	['patə]
to crease, crumple (vi)	a se şifona	[a se ʃifo'na]
to tear, to rip (vt)	a rupe	[a 'rupe]
clothes moth	molie (f)	['molie]

39. Personal care. Cosmetics

toothpaste	pastă (f) de dinţi	['pastə de dintsʲ]
toothbrush	periuţă (f) de dinţi	[peri'utse de dintsʲ]
to brush one's teeth	a se spăla pe dinţi	[a se spe'la pe dintsʲ]
razor	brici (n)	['britʃi]
shaving cream	cremă (f) de bărbierit	['kremə de bərbie'rit]
to shave (vi)	a se bărbieri	[a se bərbie'ri]
soap	săpun (n)	[sə'pun]
shampoo	şampon (n)	[ʃam'pon]
scissors	foarfece (n)	[fo'arfetʃe]
nail file	pilă (f) de unghii	['pilə de 'ungij]
nail clippers	cleştişor (n)	[kleʃti'ʃor]
tweezers	pensetă (f)	[pen'setə]

cosmetics	cosmetică (f)	[kos'metikə]
face mask	mască (f)	['maskə]
manicure	manichiură (f)	[mani'kjurə]
to have a manicure	a face manichiura	[a 'fatʃe mani'kjura]
pedicure	pedichiură (f)	[pedi'kjurə]

make-up bag	trusă (f) de cosmetică	['trusə de kos'metikə]
face powder	pudră (f)	['pudrə]
powder compact	pudrieră (f)	[pudri'erə]
blusher	fard de obraz (n)	[fard de o'braz]

perfume (bottled)	parfum (n)	[par'fum]
toilet water (lotion)	apă de toaletă (f)	['apə de toa'letə]
lotion	loțiune (f)	[loʦi'une]
cologne	colonie (f)	[ko'lonie]

eyeshadow	fard (n) de pleoape	[fard 'pentru pleo'ape]
eyeliner	creion (n) de ochi	[kre'jon 'pentru okʲ]
mascara	rimel (n)	[ri'mel]

lipstick	ruj (n)	[ruʒ]
nail polish, enamel	ojă (f)	['oʒə]
hair spray	gel (n) de păr	[dʒel de pər]
deodorant	deodorant (n)	[deodo'rant]

cream	cremă (f)	['kremə]
face cream	cremă (f) de față	['kremə de 'faʦə]
hand cream	cremă (f) pentru mâini	['kremə 'pentru mɨnʲ]
anti-wrinkle cream	cremă (f) anti-rid	['kremə 'anti rid]
day cream	cremă (f) de zi	['kremə de zi]
night cream	cremă (f) de noapte	['kremə de no'apte]
day (as adj)	de zi	[de zi]
night (as adj)	de noapte	[de no'apte]

tampon	tampon (n)	[tam'pon]
toilet paper (toilet roll)	hârtie (f) igienică	[hɨr'tie idʒi'enikə]
hair dryer	uscător (n) de păr	[uskə'tor de pər]

40. Watches. Clocks

watch (wristwatch)	ceas (n) de mână	[ʧas de 'mɨnə]
dial	cadran (n)	[ka'dran]
hand (of clock, watch)	acul (n) ceasornicului	['akul ʧasor'nikuluj]
metal watch band	brățară (f)	[brə'ʦarə]
watch strap	curea (f)	[ku'rʲa]

battery	baterie (f)	[bate'rie]
to be dead (battery)	a se termina	[a se termi'na]
to change a battery	a schimba bateria	[a skim'ba bate'rija]
to run fast	a merge înainte	[a 'merdʒe ɨna'inte]

to run slow	**a rămâne în urmă**	[a rə'mɨne ɨn 'urmə]
wall clock	**pendulă** (f)	[pen'dulə]
hourglass	**clepsidră** (f)	[klep'sidrə]
sundial	**cadran** (n) **solar**	[ka'dran so'lar]
alarm clock	**ceas** (n) **deşteptător**	[ʧas deʃteptə'tor]
watchmaker	**ceasornicar** (m)	[ʧasorni'kar]
to repair (vt)	**a repara**	[a repa'ra]

EVERYDAY EXPERIENCE

T&P Books Publishing

money	**bani** (m pl)	[banʲ]
currency exchange	**schimb** (n)	[skimb]
exchange rate	**curs** (n)	[kurs]
ATM	**bancomat** (n)	[banko'mat]
coin	**monedă** (f)	[mo'nedə]
dollar	**dolar** (m)	[do'lar]
euro	**euro** (m)	['euro]
lira	**liră** (f)	['lirə]
Deutschmark	**marcă** (f)	['markə]
franc	**franc** (m)	[frank]
pound sterling	**liră** (f) **sterlină**	['lirə ster'linə]
yen	**yen** (f)	['jen]
debt	**datorie** (f)	[dato'rie]
debtor	**datornic** (m)	[da'tornik]
to lend (money)	**a da cu împrumut**	[a da ku impru'mut]
to borrow (vi, vt)	**a lua cu împrumut**	[a lu'a ku impru'mut]
bank	**bancă** (f)	['bankə]
account	**cont** (n)	[kont]
to deposit (vt)	**a pune**	[a 'pune]
to deposit into the account	**a pune în cont**	[a 'pune in 'kont]
to withdraw (vt)	**a scoate din cont**	[a sko'ate din kont]
credit card	**carte** (f) **de credit**	['karte de 'kredit]
cash	**numerar** (n)	[nume'rar]
check	**cec** (n)	[tʃek]
to write a check	**a scrie un cec**	[a 'skrie un tʃek]
checkbook	**carte** (f) **de cecuri**	['karte de 'tʃekurʲ]
wallet	**portvizit** (n)	[portvi'zit]
change purse	**portofel** (n)	[porto'fel]
safe	**seif** (n)	['sejf]
heir	**moştenitor** (m)	[moʃteni'tor]
inheritance	**moştenire** (f)	[moʃte'nire]
fortune (wealth)	**avere** (f)	[a'vere]
lease	**arendă** (f)	[a'rendə]
rent (money)	**chirie** (f)	[ki'rie]
to rent (sth from sb)	**a închiria**	[a inkiri'ja]
price	**preţ** (n)	[prets]

| cost | valoare (f) | [valo'are] |
| sum | sumă (f) | ['sumə] |

to spend (vt)	a cheltui	[a keltu'i]
expenses	cheltuieli (f pl)	[keltu'eli]
to economize (vi, vt)	a economisi	[a ekonomi'si]
economical	econom	[eko'nom]

to pay (vi, vt)	a plăti	[a plə'ti]
payment	plată (f)	['platə]
change (give the ~)	rest (n)	[rest]

tax	impozit (n)	[im'pozit]
fine	amendă (f)	[a'mendə]
to fine (vt)	a amenda	[a amen'da]

42. Post. Postal service

post office	poştă (f)	['poʃtə]
mail (letters, etc.)	corespondenţă (f)	[korespon'dentsə]
mailman	poştaş (m)	[poʃ'taʃ]
opening hours	ore (f pl) de lucru	['ore de 'lukru]

| letter | scrisoare (f) | [skriso'are] |
| registered letter | scrisoare (f) recomandată | [skriso'are rekoman'datə] |

postcard	carte (f) poştală	['karte poʃ'talə]
telegram	telegramă (f)	[tele'gramə]
package (parcel)	colet (n)	[ko'let]
money transfer	mandat (n) poştal	[man'dat poʃ'tal]

to receive (vt)	a primi	[a pri'mi]
to send (vt)	a expedia	[a ekspedi'ja]
sending	expediere (f)	[ekspe'djere]

address	adresă (f)	[a'dresə]
ZIP code	cod (n) poştal	[kod poʃ'tal]
sender	expeditor (m)	[ekspedi'tor]
receiver	destinatar (m)	[destina'tar]

| name (first name) | prenume (n) | [pre'nume] |
| surname (last name) | nume (n) | ['nume] |

postage rate	tarif (n)	[ta'rif]
standard (adj)	normal	[nor'mal]
economical (adj)	econom	[eko'nom]

weight	greutate (f)	[greu'tate]
to weigh (~ letters)	a cântări	[a kɨntə'ri]
envelope	plic (n)	[plik]

postage stamp	**timbru** (n)	['timbru]
to stamp an envelope	**a lipi timbrul**	[a li'pi 'timbrul]

43. Banking

bank	**bancă** (f)	['bankə]
branch (of bank, etc.)	**sucursală** (f)	[sukur'salə]
bank clerk, consultant	**consultant** (m)	[konsul'tant]
manager (director)	**director** (m)	[di'rektor]
bank account	**cont** (n)	[kont]
account number	**numărul** (n) **contului**	['numərul 'kontuluj]
checking account	**cont** (n) **curent**	[kont ku'rent]
savings account	**cont** (n) **de acumulare**	[kont de akumu'lare]
to open an account	**a deschide un cont**	[a des'kide un kont]
to close the account	**a închide contul**	[a i'nkide 'kontul]
to deposit into the account	**a pune în cont**	[a 'pune in 'kont]
to withdraw (vt)	**a extrage din cont**	[a eks'tradʒe din kont]
deposit	**depozit** (n)	[de'pozit]
to make a deposit	**a depune**	[a de'pune]
wire transfer	**transfer** (n)	[trans'fer]
to wire, to transfer	**a transfera**	[a transfe'ra]
sum	**sumă** (f)	['sumə]
How much?	**Cât?**	[kit]
signature	**semnătură** (f)	[semnə'turə]
to sign (vt)	**a semna**	[a sem'na]
credit card	**carte** (f) **de credit**	['karte de 'kredit]
code (PIN code)	**cod** (n)	[kod]
credit card number	**numărul** (n) **cărţii de credit**	['numərul kərtsij de 'kredit]
ATM	**bancomat** (n)	[banko'mat]
check	**cec** (n)	[tʃek]
to write a check	**a scrie un cec**	[a 'skrie un tʃek]
checkbook	**carte** (f) **de cecuri**	['karte de 'tʃekurʲ]
loan (bank ~)	**credit** (n)	['kredit]
to apply for a loan	**a solicita un credit**	[a solitʃi'ta pe 'kredit]
to get a loan	**a lua pe credit**	[a lu'a pe 'kredit]
to give a loan	**a acorda credit**	[a akor'da 'kredit]
guarantee	**garanţie** (f)	[garan'tsie]

44. Telephone. Phone conversation

telephone	telefon (n)	[tele'fon]
cell phone	telefon (n) mobil	[tele'fon mo'bil]
answering machine	răspuns (n) automat	[rəs'puns auto'mat]
to call (by phone)	a suna, a telefona	[a su'na], [a tele'fona]
phone call	apel (n), convorbire (f)	[a'pel], [konvor'bire]
to dial a number	a forma un număr	[a for'ma un 'numər]
Hello!	Alo!	[a'lo]
to ask (vt)	a întreba	[a intre'ba]
to answer (vi, vt)	a răspunde	[a rəs'punde]
to hear (vt)	a auzi	[a au'zi]
well (adv)	bine	['bine]
not well (adv)	rău	['rəu]
noises (interference)	bruiaj (n)	[bru'jaʒ]
receiver	receptor (n)	[retʃep'tor]
to pick up (~ the phone)	a lua receptorul	[a lu'a retʃep'torul]
to hang up (~ the phone)	a pune receptorul	[a 'pune retʃep'torul]
busy (engaged)	ocupat	[oku'pat]
to ring (ab. phone)	a suna	[a su'na]
telephone book	carte (f) de telefon	['karte de tele'fon]
local (adj)	local	[lo'kal]
local call	apel (n) local	[a'pel lo'kal]
long distance (~ call)	interurban	[interur'ban]
long-distance call	apel (n) interurban	[a'pel interur'ban]
international (adj)	internațional	[internatsio'nal]
international call	apel (n) interna ional	[a'pel internatsio'nal]

45. Cell phone

cell phone	telefon (n) mobil	[tele'fon mo'bil]
display	ecran (n)	[e'kran]
button	buton (n)	[bu'ton]
SIM card	cartelă (f) SIM	[kar'telə 'sim]
battery	baterie (f)	[bate'rie]
to be dead (battery)	a se descărca	[a se deskər'ka]
charger	încărcător (m)	[inkərkə'tor]
menu	meniu (n)	[me'nju]
settings	setări (f)	[se'tərʲ]
tune (melody)	melodie (f)	[melo'die]
to select (vt)	a selecta	[a selek'ta]

calculator	calculator (n)	[kalkula'tor]
voice mail	răspuns (n) automat	[res'puns auto'mat]
alarm clock	ceas (n) deşteptător	[tʃas deʃteptə'tor]
contacts	carte (f) de telefoane	['karte de telefo'ane]

| SMS (text message) | SMS (n) | [ese'mes] |
| subscriber | abonat (m) | [abo'nat] |

46. Stationery

| ballpoint pen | stilou (n) | [sti'lou] |
| fountain pen | condei (n) | [kon'dej] |

pencil	creion (n)	[kre'jon]
highlighter	marcher (n)	['marker]
felt-tip pen	carioca (f)	[kari'okə]

| notepad | carneţel (n) | [karne'tsəl] |
| agenda (diary) | agendă (f) | [a'dʒendə] |

ruler	riglă (f)	['riglə]
calculator	calculator (f)	[kalkula'tor]
eraser	radieră (f)	[radi'erə]
thumbtack	piuneză (f)	[pju'nezə]
paper clip	clamă (f)	['klamə]

glue	lipici (n)	[li'pitʃi]
stapler	capsator (n)	[kapsa'tor]
hole punch	perforator (n)	[perfo'rator]
pencil sharpener	ascuţitoare (f)	[askutsito'are]

47. Foreign languages

language	limbă (f)	['limbə]
foreign (adj)	străin	[stre'in]
foreign language	limbă (f) străină	['limbə stre'inə]
to study (vt)	a studia	[a studi'a]
to learn (language, etc.)	a învăţa	[a inve'tsa]

to read (vi, vt)	a citi	[a tʃi'ti]
to speak (vi, vt)	a vorbi	[a vor'bi]
to understand (vt)	a înţelege	[a intse'ledʒe]
to write (vt)	a scrie	[a 'skrie]

fast (adv)	repede	['repede]
slowly (adv)	încet	[in'tʃet]
fluently (adv)	liber	['liber]
rules	reguli (f pl)	['reguli]

grammar	gramatică (f)	[gra'matikə]
vocabulary	lexic (n)	['leksik]
phonetics	fonetică (f)	[fo'netikə]

textbook	manual (n)	[manu'al]
dictionary	dicționar (n)	[diktsio'nar]
teach-yourself book	manual (n) autodidactic	[manu'al autodi'daktik]
phrasebook	ghid (n) de conversație	[gid de konver'satsie]

cassette, tape	casetă (f)	[ka'setə]
videotape	casetă (f) video	[ka'setə 'video]
CD, compact disc	CD (n)	[si'di]
DVD	DVD (n)	[divi'di]

alphabet	alfabet (n)	[alfa'bet]
to spell (vt)	a spune pe litere	[a vor'bi pe 'litere]
pronunciation	pronunție (f)	[pro'nuntsie]

accent	accent (n)	[ak'tʃent]
with an accent	cu accent	['ku ak'tʃent]
without an accent	fără accent	['fərə ak'tʃent]

| word | cuvânt (n) | [ku'vint] |
| meaning | sens (n) | [sens] |

course (e.g., a French ~)	cursuri (n)	['kursurʲ]
to sign up	a se înscrie	[a se in'skrie]
teacher	profesor (m)	[pro'fesor]

translation (process)	traducere (f)	[tra'dutʃere]
translation (text, etc.)	traducere (f)	[tra'dutʃere]
translator	traducător (m)	[traduke'tor]
interpreter	translator (m)	[trans'lator]

| polyglot | poliglot (m) | [poli'glot] |
| memory | memorie (f) | [me'morie] |

MEALS. RESTAURANT

T&P Books Publishing

48. Table setting

spoon	**lingură** (f)	['lingurə]
knife	**cuțit** (n)	[ku'tsit]
fork	**furculiță** (f)	[furku'litsə]
cup (e.g., coffee ~)	**ceașcă** (f)	['tʃaʃkə]
plate (dinner ~)	**farfurie** (f)	[farfu'rie]
saucer	**farfurioară** (f)	[farfurio'arə]
napkin (on table)	**șervețel** (n)	[ʃerve'tsel]
toothpick	**scobitoare** (f)	[skobito'are]

49. Restaurant

restaurant	**restaurant** (n)	[restau'rant]
coffee house	**cafenea** (f)	[kafe'nʲa]
pub, bar	**bar** (n)	[bar]
tearoom	**salon** (n) **de ceai**	[sa'lon de tʃaj]
waiter	**chelner** (m)	['kelner]
waitress	**chelneriță** (f)	[kelne'ritsə]
bartender	**barman** (m)	['barman]
menu	**meniu** (n)	[me'nju]
wine list	**meniu** (n) **de vinuri**	[menju de 'vinurʲ]
to book a table	**a rezerva o masă**	[a rezer'va o 'masə]
course, dish	**mâncare** (f)	[mɨn'kare]
to order (meal)	**a comanda**	[a koman'da]
to make an order	**a face comandă**	[a 'fatʃe ko'mandə]
aperitif	**aperitiv** (n)	[aperi'tiv]
appetizer	**gustare** (f)	[gus'tare]
dessert	**desert** (n)	[de'sert]
check	**notă** (f) **de plată**	['notə de 'platə]
to pay the check	**a achita nota de plată**	[a aki'ta 'nota de 'platə]
to give change	**a da rest**	[a da 'rest]
tip	**bacșiș** (n)	[bak'ʃiʃ]

50. Meals

food	**mâncare** (f)	[mɨn'kare]
to eat (vi, vt)	**a mânca**	[a mɨn'ka]

breakfast	micul dejun (n)	['mikul de'ʒun]
to have breakfast	a lua micul dejun	[a lu'a 'mikul de'ʒun]
lunch	prânz (n)	[prɨnz]
to have lunch	a lua prânzul	[a lu'a 'prɨnzul]
dinner	cină (f)	['tʃinə]
to have dinner	a cina	[a tʃi'na]
appetite	poftă (f) de mâncare	['poftə de mɨ'nkare]
Enjoy your meal!	Poftă bună!	['poftə 'bunə]
to open (~ a bottle)	a deschide	[a des'kide]
to spill (liquid)	a vărsa	[a vər'sa]
to spill out (vi)	a se vărsa	[a se vər'sa]
to boil (vi)	a fierbe	[a 'fjerbe]
to boil (vt)	a fierbe	[a 'fjerbe]
boiled (~ water)	fiert	[fiert]
to chill, cool down (vt)	a răci	[a rə'tʃi]
to chill (vi)	a se răci	[a se rə'tʃi]
taste, flavor	gust (n)	[gust]
aftertaste	aromă (f)	[a'romə]
to slim down (lose weight)	a slăbi	[a slə'bi]
diet	dietă (f)	[di'etə]
vitamin	vitamină (f)	[vita'minə]
calorie	calorie (f)	[kalo'rie]
vegetarian (n)	vegetarian (m)	[vedʒetari'an]
vegetarian (adj)	vegetarian	[vedʒetari'an]
fats (nutrient)	grăsimi (f pl)	[grə'simʲ]
proteins	proteine (f pl)	[prote'ine]
carbohydrates	hidrați (m pl) de carbon	[hi'dratsʲ de kar'bon]
slice (of lemon, ham)	felie (f)	[fe'lie]
piece (of cake, pie)	bucată (f)	[bu'katə]
crumb (of bread, cake, etc.)	firimitură (f)	[firimi'turə]

51. Cooked dishes

course, dish	fel (n) de mâncare	[fel de mɨ'nkare]
cuisine	bucătărie (f)	[bukətə'rie]
recipe	rețetă (f)	[re'tsetə]
portion	porție (f)	['portsie]
salad	salată (f)	[sa'latə]
soup	supă (f)	['supə]
clear soup (broth)	supă (f) de carne	['supə de 'karne]
sandwich (bread)	tartină (f)	[tar'tinə]

fried eggs	omletă (f)	[om'letə]
hamburger (beefburger)	hamburger (m)	['hamburger]
beefsteak	biftec (n)	[bif'tek]

side dish	garnitură (f)	[garni'turə]
spaghetti	spaghete (f pl)	[spa'gete]
mashed potatoes	piure (n) de cartofi	[pju're de kar'tofʲ]
pizza	pizza (f)	['pitsa]
porridge (oatmeal, etc.)	caşă (f)	['kaʃə]
omelet	omletă (f)	[om'letə]

boiled (e.g., ~ beef)	fiert	[fiert]
smoked (adj)	afumat	[afu'mat]
fried (adj)	prăjit	[prə'ʒit]
dried (adj)	uscat	[us'kat]
frozen (adj)	congelat	[kondʒe'lat]
pickled (adj)	marinat	[mari'nat]

sweet (sugary)	dulce	['dultʃe]
salty (adj)	sărat	[sə'rat]
cold (adj)	rece	['retʃe]
hot (adj)	fierbinte	[fier'binte]
bitter (adj)	amar	[a'mar]
tasty (adj)	gustos	[gus'tos]

to cook in boiling water	a fierbe	[a 'fjerbe]
to cook (dinner)	a găti	[a gə'ti]
to fry (vt)	a prăji	[a prə'ʒi]
to heat up (food)	a încălzi	[a ɨnkəl'zi]

to salt (vt)	a săra	[a sə'ra]
to pepper (vt)	a pipera	[a pipe'ra]
to grate (vt)	a da prin răzătoare	[a da prin rəzəto'are]
peel (n)	coajă (f)	[ko'aʒə]
to peel (vt)	a curăţa	[a kurə'tsa]

52. Food

meat	carne (f)	['karne]
chicken	carne (f) de găină	['karne de gə'inə]
Rock Cornish hen (poussin)	carne (f) de pui	['karne de puj]
duck	carne (f) de raţă	['karne de 'ratsə]
goose	carne (f) de gâscă	['karne de 'gɨskə]
game	vânat (n)	[vɨ'nat]
turkey	carne (f) de curcan	['karne de 'kurkan]
pork	carne (f) de porc	['karne de pork]
veal	carne (f) de viţel	['karne de vi'tsel]
lamb	carne (f) de berbec	['karne de ber'bek]

beef	carne (f) de vită	['karne de 'vitə]
rabbit	carne (f) de iepure de casă	['karne de 'epure de 'kasə]

sausage (bologna, etc.)	salam (n)	[sa'lam]
vienna sausage (frankfurter)	crenvurşt (n)	[kren'vurʃt]
bacon	costiță (f) afumată	[kos'titsə afu'matə]
ham	şuncă (f)	['ʃunkə]
gammon	pulpă (f)	['pulpə]

pâté	pateu (n)	[pa'teu]
liver	ficat (m)	[fi'kat]
hamburger (ground beef)	carne (f) tocată	['karne to'katə]
tongue	limbă (f)	['limbə]

egg	ou (n)	['ow]
eggs	ouă (n pl)	['owə]
egg white	albuş (n)	[al'buʃ]
egg yolk	gălbenuş	[gəlbe'nuʃ]

fish	peşte (m)	['peʃte]
seafood	produse (n pl) marine	[pro'duse ma'rine]
caviar	icre (f pl) de peşte	['ikre de 'peʃte]

crab	crab (m)	[krab]
shrimp	crevetă (f)	[kre'vetə]
oyster	stridie (f)	['stridie]
spiny lobster	langustă (f)	[lan'gustə]
octopus	caracatiță (f)	[kara'katitsə]
squid	calmar (m)	[kal'mar]

sturgeon	carne (f) de nisetru	['karne de ni'setru]
salmon	somon (m)	[so'mon]
halibut	calcan (m)	[kal'kan]

cod	batog (m)	[ba'tog]
mackerel	macrou (n)	[ma'krou]
tuna	ton (m)	[ton]
eel	ţipar (m)	[tsi'par]

trout	păstrăv (m)	[pəs'trəv]
sardine	sardea (f)	[sar'dia]
pike	ştiucă (f)	['ʃtjukə]
herring	scrumbie (f)	[skrum'bie]

bread	pâine (f)	['pɨne]
cheese	caşcaval (n)	['brinzə]
sugar	zahăr (n)	['zahər]
salt	sare (f)	['sare]
rice	orez (n)	[o'rez]
pasta (macaroni)	paste (f pl)	['paste]

noodles	tăiţei (m)	[təi'tsej]
butter	unt (n)	['unt]
vegetable oil	ulei (n) vegetal	[u'lej vedʒe'tal]
sunflower oil	ulei (n) de floarea-soarelui	[u'lej de flo'arʲa so'areluj]
margarine	margarină (f)	[marga'rinə]

| olives | olive (f pl) | [o'live] |
| olive oil | ulei (n) de măsline | [u'lej de məs'line] |

milk	lapte (n)	['lapte]
condensed milk	lapte (n) condensat	['lapte konden'sat]
yogurt	iaurt (n)	[ja'urt]
sour cream	smântână (f)	[smɨn'tɨnə]
cream (of milk)	frişcă (f)	['friʃkə]

| mayonnaise | maioneză (f) | [majo'nezə] |
| buttercream | cremă (f) | ['kremə] |

groats (barley ~, etc.)	crupe (f pl)	['krupe]
flour	făină (f)	[fə'inə]
canned food	conserve (f pl)	[kon'serve]

cornflakes	fulgi (m pl) de porumb	['fuldʒʲ de po'rumb]
honey	miere (f)	['mjere]
jam	gem (n)	[dʒem]
chewing gum	gumă (f) de mestecat	['gumə de meste'kat]

53. Drinks

water	apă (f)	['apə]
drinking water	apă (f) potabilă	['apə po'tabilə]
mineral water	apă (f) minerală	['apə mine'ralə]

still (adj)	necarbogazoasă	[nekarbogazo'asə]
carbonated (adj)	carbogazoasă	[karbogazo'asə]
sparkling (adj)	gazoasă	[gazo'asə]
ice	gheaţă (f)	['gʲatsə]
with ice	cu gheaţă	[ku 'gʲatsə]

non-alcoholic (adj)	fără alcool	['fərə alko'ol]
soft drink	băutură (f) fără alcool	[bəu'turə fərə alko'ol]
refreshing drink	băutură (f) răcoritoare	[bəu'turə rəkorito'are]
lemonade	limonadă (f)	[limo'nadə]

liquors	băuturi (f pl) alcoolice	[bəu'turʲ alko'olitʃe]
wine	vin (n)	[vin]
white wine	vin (n) alb	[vin alb]
red wine	vin (n) roşu	[vin 'roʃu]
liqueur	lichior (n)	[li'kør]

| champagne | şampanie (f) | [ʃam'panie] |
| vermouth | vermut (n) | [ver'mut] |

whiskey	whisky (n)	['wiski]
vodka	votcă (f)	['votkə]
gin	gin (n)	[ʤin]
cognac	coniac (n)	[ko'njak]
rum	rom (n)	[rom]

coffee	cafea (f)	[ka'fʲa]
black coffee	cafea (f) neagră	[ka'fʲa 'nʲagrə]
coffee with milk	cafea (f) cu lapte	[ka'fʲa ku 'lapte]
cappuccino	cafea (f) cu frişcă	[ka'fʲa ku 'friʃkə]
instant coffee	cafea (f) solubilă	[ka'fʲa so'lubilə]

milk	lapte (n)	['lapte]
cocktail	cocteil (n)	[kok'tejl]
milkshake	cocteil (n) din lapte	[kok'tejl din 'lapte]

juice	suc (n)	[suk]
tomato juice	suc (n) de roşii	[suk de 'roʃij]
orange juice	suc (n) de portocale	[suk de porto'kale]
freshly squeezed juice	suc (n) natural	[suk natu'ral]

beer	bere (f)	['bere]
light beer	bere (f) blondă	['bere 'blondə]
dark beer	bere (f) brună	['bere 'brunə]

tea	ceai (n)	[ʧaj]
black tea	ceai (n) negru	[ʧaj 'negru]
green tea	ceai (n) verde	[ʧaj 'verde]

54. Vegetables

| vegetables | legume (f pl) | [le'gume] |
| greens | verdeaţă (f) | [ver'dʲaʦə] |

tomato	roşie (f)	['roʃie]
cucumber	castravete (m)	[kastra'vete]
carrot	morcov (m)	['morkov]
potato	cartof (m)	[kar'tof]
onion	ceapă (f)	['ʧapə]
garlic	usturoi (m)	[ustu'roj]

cabbage	varză (f)	['varzə]
cauliflower	conopidă (f)	[kono'pidə]
Brussels sprouts	varză (f) de Bruxelles	['varze de bruk'sel]
broccoli	broccoli (m)	['brokoli]
beet	sfeclă (f)	['sfeklə]
eggplant	pătlăgea (f) vânătă	[pətlə'ʤʲa 'vɨnətə]

zucchini	dovlecel (m)	[dovle'tʃel]
pumpkin	dovleac (m)	[dov'lʲak]
turnip	nap (m)	[nap]

parsley	pătrunjel (m)	[pətrun'ʒel]
dill	mărar (m)	[mə'rar]
lettuce	salată (f)	[sa'latə]
celery	ţelină (f)	['tselinə]
asparagus	sparanghel (m)	[sparan'gel]
spinach	spanac (n)	[spa'nak]

pea	mazăre (f)	['mazəre]
beans	boabe (f pl)	[bo'abe]
corn (maize)	porumb (m)	[po'rumb]
kidney bean	fasole (f)	[fa'sole]

bell pepper	piper (m)	[pi'per]
radish	ridiche (f)	[ri'dike]
artichoke	anghinare (f)	[angi'nare]

55. Fruits. Nuts

fruit	fruct (n)	[frukt]
apple	măr (n)	[mər]
pear	pară (f)	['parə]
lemon	lămâie (f)	[lə'mie]
orange	portocală (f)	[porto'kalə]
strawberry (garden ~)	căpşună (f)	[kəp'ʃunə]

mandarin	mandarină (f)	[manda'rinə]
plum	prună (f)	['prunə]
peach	piersică (f)	['pjersikə]
apricot	caisă (f)	[ka'isə]
raspberry	zmeură (f)	['zmeurə]
pineapple	ananas (m)	[ana'nas]

banana	banană (f)	[ba'nanə]
watermelon	pepene (m) verde	['pepene 'verde]
grape	struguri (m pl)	['strugurʲ]
sour cherry	vişină (f)	['viʃinə]
sweet cherry	cireaşă (f)	[tʃi'rʲaʃə]
melon	pepene (m) galben	['pepene 'galben]

grapefruit	grepfrut (n)	['grepfrut]
avocado	avocado (n)	[avo'kado]
papaya	papaia (f)	[pa'paja]
mango	mango (n)	['mango]
pomegranate	rodie (f)	['rodie]
redcurrant	coacăză (f) roşie	[ko'akəzə 'roʃie]
blackcurrant	coacăză (f) neagră	[ko'akəzə 'nʲagrə]

gooseberry	**agrişă** (f)	[a'griʃə]
bilberry	**afină** (f)	[a'finə]
blackberry	**mură** (f)	['murə]

raisin	**stafidă** (f)	[sta'fidə]
fig	**smochină** (f)	[smo'kinə]
date	**curmală** (f)	[kur'malə]

peanut	**arahidă** (f)	[ara'hidə]
almond	**migdală** (f)	[mig'dalə]
walnut	**nucă** (f)	['nukə]
hazelnut	**alună** (f) **de pădure**	[a'lunə de pə'dure]
coconut	**nucă** (f) **de cocos**	['nukə de 'kokos]
pistachios	**fistic** (m)	['fistik]

56. Bread. Candy

bakers' confectionery (pastry)	**produse** (n pl) **de cofetărie**	[pro'duse də kofetə'rie]
bread	**pâine** (f)	['pɨne]
cookies	**biscuit** (m)	[bisku'it]

chocolate (n)	**ciocolată** (f)	[tʃioko'latə]
chocolate (as adj)	**de, din ciocolată**	[de, din tʃioko'latə]
candy (wrapped)	**bomboană** (f)	[bombo'anə]
cake (e.g., cupcake)	**prăjitură** (f)	[prəʒi'turə]
cake (e.g., birthday ~)	**tort** (n)	[tort]

| pie (e.g., apple ~) | **plăcintă** (f) | [plə'tʃintə] |
| filling (for cake, pie) | **umplutură** (f) | [umplu'turə] |

jam (whole fruit jam)	**dulceaţă** (f)	[dul'tʃatsə]
marmalade	**marmeladă** (f)	[marme'ladə]
wafers	**napolitane** (f pl)	[napoli'tane]
ice-cream	**îngheţată** (f)	[ɨnge'tsatə]

57. Spices

salt	**sare** (f)	['sare]
salty (adj)	**sărat**	[sə'rat]
to salt (vt)	**a săra**	[a sə'ra]

black pepper	**piper** (m) **negru**	[pi'per 'negru]
red pepper (milled ~)	**piper** (m) **roşu**	[pi'per 'roʃu]
mustard	**muştar** (m)	[muʃ'tar]
horseradish	**hrean** (n)	[hr'an]
condiment	**condiment** (n)	[kondi'ment]
spice	**condiment** (n)	[kondi'ment]

sauce	**sos** (n)	[sos]
vinegar	**oţet** (n)	[o'tset]
anise	**anason** (m)	[ana'son]
basil	**busuioc** (n)	[busu'jok]
cloves	**cuişoare** (f pl)	[kuiʃo'are]
ginger	**ghimber** (m)	[gim'ber]
coriander	**coriandru** (m)	[kori'andru]
cinnamon	**scorţişoară** (f)	[skortsiʃo'arə]
sesame	**susan** (m)	[su'san]
bay leaf	**foi** (f) **de dafin**	[foj de 'dafin]
paprika	**paprică** (f)	['paprikə]
caraway	**chimen** (m)	[ki'men]
saffron	**şofran** (m)	[ʃo'fran]

PERSONAL
INFORMATION. FAMILY

T&P Books Publishing

58. Personal information. Forms

name (first name)	**prenume** (n)	[pre'nume]
surname (last name)	**nume** (n)	['nume]
date of birth	**data** (f) **naşterii**	['data 'naʃterij]
place of birth	**locul** (n) **naşterii**	['lokul 'naʃterij]
nationality	**naţionalitate** (f)	[natsionali'tate]
place of residence	**locul** (n) **de reşedinţă**	['lokul de reʃə'dintsə]
country	**ţară** (f)	['tsarə]
profession (occupation)	**profesie** (f)	[pro'fesie]
gender, sex	**sex** (n)	[seks]
height	**înălţime** (f)	[inəl'tsime]
weight	**greutate** (f)	[greu'tate]

59. Family members. Relatives

mother	**mamă** (f)	['mamə]
father	**tată** (m)	['tatə]
son	**fiu** (m)	['fju]
daughter	**fiică** (f)	['fiikə]
younger daughter	**fiica** (f) **mai mică**	['fiika maj 'mikə]
younger son	**fiul** (m) **mai mic**	['fjul maj mik]
eldest daughter	**fiica** (f) **mai mare**	['fiika maj 'mare]
eldest son	**fiul** (m) **mai mare**	['fjul maj 'mare]
brother	**frate** (m)	['frate]
elder brother	**frate** (m) **mai mare**	['frate maj 'mare]
younger brother	**frate** (m) **mai mic**	['frate maj mik]
sister	**soră** (f)	['sorə]
elder sister	**soră** (f) **mai mare**	['sorə maj 'mare]
younger sister	**soră** (f) **mai mică**	['sorə maj 'mikə]
cousin (masc.)	**văr** (m)	[vər]
cousin (fem.)	**vară** (f)	['varə]
mom, mommy	**mamă** (f)	['mamə]
dad, daddy	**tată** (m)	['tatə]
parents	**părinţi** (m pl)	[pə'rintsʲ]
child	**copil** (m)	[ko'pil]
children	**copii** (m pl)	[ko'pij]
grandmother	**bunică** (f)	[bu'nikə]
grandfather	**bunic** (m)	[bu'nik]

grandson	nepot (m)	[ne'pot]
granddaughter	nepoată (f)	[nepo'atə]
grandchildren	nepoți (m pl)	[ne'potsʲ]
uncle	unchi (m)	[unkʲ]
aunt	mătușă (f)	[mə'tuʃə]
nephew	nepot (m)	[ne'pot]
niece	nepoată (f)	[nepo'atə]
mother-in-law (wife's mother)	soacră (f)	[so'akrə]
father-in-law (husband's father)	socru (m)	['sokru]
son-in-law (daughter's husband)	cumnat (m)	[kum'nat]
stepmother	mamă vitregă (f)	['mamə 'vitregə]
stepfather	tată vitreg (m)	['tatə 'vitreg]
infant	sugaci (m)	[su'gatʃi]
baby (infant)	prunc (m)	[prunk]
little boy, kid	pici (m)	[pitʃi]
wife	soție (f)	[so'tsie]
husband	soț (m)	[sots]
spouse (husband)	soț (m)	[sots]
spouse (wife)	soție (f)	[so'tsie]
married (masc.)	căsătorit	[kəsəto'rit]
married (fem.)	căsătorită	[kəsəto'ritə]
single (unmarried)	celibatar (m)	[tʃeliba'tar]
bachelor	burlac (m)	[bur'lak]
divorced (masc.)	divorțat	[divor'tsat]
widow	văduvă (f)	[vəduvə]
widower	văduv (m)	[vəduv]
relative	rudă (f)	['rudə]
close relative	rudă (f) apropiată	['rudə apropi'jatə]
distant relative	rudă (f) îndepărtată	['rudə indepər'tatə]
relatives	rude (f pl) de sânge	['rude de 'sindʒe]
orphan (boy or girl)	orfan (m)	[or'fan]
guardian (of a minor)	tutore (m)	[tu'tore]
to adopt (a boy)	a adopta	[a adop'ta]
to adopt (a girl)	a adopta	[a adop'ta]

60. Friends. Coworkers

friend (masc.)	prieten (m)	[pri'eten]
friend (fem.)	prietenă (f)	[pri'etenə]
friendship	prietenie (f)	[priete'nie]

to be friends	**a prieteni**	[a prieteˈni]
buddy (masc.)	**amic** (m)	[aˈmik]
buddy (fem.)	**amică** (f)	[aˈmikə]
partner	**partener** (m)	[parteˈner]

chief (boss)	**şef** (m)	[ʃef]
superior (n)	**director** (m)	[diˈrektor]
owner, proprietor	**proprietar** (m)	[proprieˈtar]
subordinate (n)	**subordonat** (m)	[subordoˈnat]
colleague	**coleg** (m)	[koˈleg]

acquaintance (person)	**cunoscut** (m)	[kunosˈkut]
fellow traveler	**tovarăş** (m) **de drum**	[toˈvarəʃ de drum]
classmate	**coleg** (m) **de clasă**	[koˈleg de ˈklasə]

neighbor (masc.)	**vecin** (m)	[veˈʧin]
neighbor (fem.)	**vecină** (f)	[veˈʧinə]
neighbors	**vecini** (m pl)	[veˈʧinʲ]

HUMAN BODY. MEDICINE

T&P Books Publishing

61. Head

head	**cap** (n)	[kap]
face	**față** (f)	['fatsə]
nose	**nas** (n)	[nas]
mouth	**gură** (f)	['gurə]
eye	**ochi** (m)	[okʲ]
eyes	**ochi** (m pl)	[okʲ]
pupil	**pupilă** (f)	[pu'pilə]
eyebrow	**sprânceană** (f)	[sprin'tʃanə]
eyelash	**geană** (f)	['dʒanə]
eyelid	**pleoapă** (f)	[pleo'apə]
tongue	**limbă** (f)	['limbə]
tooth	**dinte** (m)	['dinte]
lips	**buze** (f pl)	['buze]
cheekbones	**pomeți** (m pl)	[po'metsʲ]
gum	**gingie** (f)	[dʒin'dʒie]
palate	**palat** (n)	[pa'lat]
nostrils	**nări** (f pl)	[nərʲ]
chin	**bărbie** (f)	[bər'bie]
jaw	**maxilar** (n)	[maksi'lar]
cheek	**obraz** (m)	[o'braz]
forehead	**frunte** (f)	['frunte]
temple	**tâmplă** (f)	['tɨmplə]
ear	**ureche** (f)	[u'reke]
back of the head	**ceafă** (f)	['tʃafə]
neck	**gât** (n)	[gɨt]
throat	**gât** (n)	[gɨt]
hair	**păr** (m)	[pər]
hairstyle	**coafură** (f)	[koa'furə]
haircut	**tunsoare** (f)	[tunso'are]
wig	**perucă** (f)	[pe'rukə]
mustache	**mustăți** (f pl)	[mus'tətsʲ]
beard	**barbă** (f)	['barbə]
to have (a beard, etc.)	**a purta**	[a pur'ta]
braid	**cosiță** (f)	[ko'sitsə]
sideburns	**favoriți** (m pl)	[favo'ritsʲ]
red-haired (adj)	**roșcat**	[roʃ'kat]
gray (hair)	**cărunt**	[kə'runt]

| bald (adj) | chel | [kel] |
| bald patch | chelie (f) | [ke'lie] |

| ponytail | coadă (f) | [ko'adə] |
| bangs | breton (n) | [bre'ton] |

62. Human body

| hand | mână (f) | ['mɨnə] |
| arm | braț (n) | [brats] |

finger	deget (n)	['dedʒet]
toe	deget (n) de la picior	['dedʒet de la pi'tʃior]
thumb	degetul (n) mare	['dedʒetul 'mare]
little finger	degetul (n) mic	['dedʒetul mik]
nail	unghie (f)	['ungie]

fist	pumn (m)	[pumn]
palm	palmă (f)	['palmə]
wrist	încheietura (f) mâinii	[ɨnkeje'tura 'mɨnij]
forearm	antebraț (n)	[ante'brats]
elbow	cot (n)	[kot]
shoulder	umăr (m)	['umər]

leg	picior (n)	[pi'tʃior]
foot	talpă (f)	['talpə]
knee	genunchi (n)	[dʒe'nunkʲ]
calf (part of leg)	pulpă (f)	['pulpə]
hip	coapsă (f)	[ko'apsə]
heel	călcâi (n)	[kəl'kɨj]

body	corp (n)	[korp]
stomach	burtă (f)	['burtə]
chest	piept (n)	[pjept]
breast	sân (m)	[sɨn]
flank	coastă (f)	[ko'astə]
back	spate (n)	['spate]

| lower back | regiune (f) lombară | [redʒi'une lom'barə] |
| waist | talie (f) | ['talie] |

navel (belly button)	buric (n)	[bu'rik]
buttocks	fese (f pl)	['fese]
bottom	şezut (n)	[ʃe'zut]

beauty mark	aluniță (f)	[alu'nitsə]
birthmark (café au lait spot)	semn (n) din naştere	[semn din 'naʃtere]
tattoo	tatuaj (n)	[tatu'aʒ]
scar	cicatrice (f)	[tʃika'tritʃe]

63. Diseases

sickness	boală (f)	[bo'alə]
to be sick	a fi bolnav	[a fi bol'nav]
health	sănătate (f)	[sənə'tate]
runny nose (coryza)	guturai (n)	[gutu'raj]
tonsillitis	anghină (f)	[a'nginə]
cold (illness)	răceală (f)	[rə'tʃalə]
to catch a cold	a răci	[a rə'tʃi]
bronchitis	bronşită (f)	[bron'ʃitə]
pneumonia	pneumonie (f)	[pneumo'nie]
flu, influenza	gripă (f)	['gripə]
nearsighted (adj)	miop	[mi'op]
farsighted (adj)	prezbit	[prez'bit]
strabismus (crossed eyes)	strabism (n)	[stra'bism]
cross-eyed (adj)	saşiu	[sa'ʃiu]
cataract	cataractă (f)	[kata'raktə]
glaucoma	glaucom (n)	[glau'kom]
stroke	congestie (f)	[kon'dʒestie]
heart attack	infarct (n)	[in'farkt]
myocardial infarction	infarct (n) miocardic	[in'farkt mio'kardik]
paralysis	paralizie (f)	[parali'zie]
to paralyze (vt)	a paraliza	[a parali'za]
allergy	alergie (f)	[aler'dʒie]
asthma	astmă (f)	['astmə]
diabetes	diabet (n)	[dia'bet]
toothache	durere (f) de dinţi	[du'rere de dints]
caries	carie (f)	['karie]
diarrhea	diaree (f)	[dia'ree]
constipation	constipaţie (f)	[konsti'patsie]
stomach upset	deranjament (n) la stomac	[deranʒa'ment la sto'mak]
food poisoning	intoxicare (f)	[intoksi'kare]
to get food poisoning	a se intoxica	[a se intoksi'ka]
arthritis	artrită (f)	[ar'tritə]
rickets	rahitism (n)	[rahi'tism]
rheumatism	reumatism (n)	[reuma'tism]
atherosclerosis	ateroscleroză (f)	[arterioskle'rozə]
gastritis	gastrită (f)	[gas'tritə]
appendicitis	apendicită (f)	[apendi'tʃitə]
cholecystitis	colecistită (f)	[koletʃis'titə]
ulcer	ulcer (n)	[ul'tʃer]

measles	pojar	[po'ʒar]
rubella (German measles)	rubeolă (f)	[ruʒe'ole]
jaundice	icter (n)	['ikter]
hepatitis	hepatită (f)	[hepa'titə]

schizophrenia	schizofrenie (f)	[skizofre'nie]
rabies (hydrophobia)	turbare (f)	[tur'bare]
neurosis	nevroză (f)	[ne'vroze]
concussion	comoție (f) cerebrală	[ko'motsie tʃere'brale]

cancer	cancer (n)	['kantʃer]
sclerosis	scleroză (f)	[skle'roze]
multiple sclerosis	scleroză multiplă (f)	[skle'roze mul'tiple]

alcoholism	alcoolism (n)	[alkoo'lizm]
alcoholic (n)	alcoolic (m)	[alko'olik]
syphilis	sifilis (n)	['sifilis]
AIDS	SIDA (f)	['sida]

tumor	tumoare (f)	[tumo'are]
malignant (adj)	malignă	[ma'ligne]
benign (adj)	benignă	[be'nigne]

fever	friguri (n pl)	['friguri]
malaria	malarie (f)	[mala'rie]
gangrene	cangrenă (f)	[kan'grene]
seasickness	rău (n) de mare	[reu de 'mare]
epilepsy	epilepsie (f)	[epilep'sie]

epidemic	epidemie (f)	[epide'mie]
typhus	tifos (n)	['tifos]
tuberculosis	tuberculoză (f)	[tuberku'loze]
cholera	holeră (f)	['holere]
plague (bubonic ~)	ciumă (f)	['tʃiume]

64. Symptoms. Treatments. Part 1

symptom	simptom (n)	[simp'tom]
temperature	temperatură (f)	[tempera'ture]
high temperature (fever)	febră (f)	['febre]
pulse (heartbeat)	puls (n)	[puls]

dizziness (vertigo)	amețeală (f)	[ame'tsiale]
hot (adj)	fierbinte	[fier'binte]
shivering	frisoane (n pl)	[friso'ane]
pale (e.g., ~ face)	palid	['palid]

cough	tuse (f)	['tuse]
to cough (vi)	a tuşi	[a tu'ʃi]
to sneeze (vi)	a strănuta	[a strenu'ta]

| faint | leşin (n) | [le'ʃin] |
| to faint (vi) | a leşina | [a leʃi'na] |

bruise (hématome)	vânătaie (f)	[vɨnə'tae]
bump (lump)	cucui (n)	[ku'kuj]
to bang (bump)	a se lovi	[a se lo'vi]
contusion (bruise)	contuzie (f)	[kon'tuzie]
to get a bruise	a se lovi	[a se lo'vi]

to limp (vi)	a şchiopăta	[a ʃkiopə'ta]
dislocation	luxaţie (f)	[luk'satsie]
to dislocate (vt)	a luxa	[a luk'sa]
fracture	fractură (f)	[frak'turə]
to have a fracture	a fractura	[a fraktu'ra]

cut (e.g., paper ~)	tăietură (f)	[təe'turə]
to cut oneself	a se tăia	[a se tə'ja]
bleeding	sângerare (f)	[sɨndʒe'rare]

| burn (injury) | arsură (f) | [ar'surə] |
| to get burned | a se frige | [a se 'fridʒe] |

to prick (vt)	a înţepa	[a ɨntse'pa]
to prick oneself	a se înţepa	[a s ɨntse'pa]
to injure (vt)	a se răni	[a se rə'ni]
injury	vătămare (f)	[vətə'mare]
wound	rană (f)	['ranə]
trauma	traumă (f)	['traumə]

to be delirious	a delira	[a deli'ra]
to stutter (vi)	a se bâlbâi	[a se bɨlbɨ'i]
sunstroke	insolaţie (f)	[inso'latsie]

65. Symptoms. Treatments. Part 2

| pain, ache | durere (f) | [du'rere] |
| splinter (in foot, etc.) | ghimpe (m) | ['gimpe] |

sweat (perspiration)	transpiraţie (f)	[transpi'ratsie]
to sweat (perspire)	a transpira	[a transpi'ra]
vomiting	vomă (f)	['vomə]
convulsions	convulsii (f pl)	[kon'vulsij]

pregnant (adj)	gravidă (f)	[gra'vidə]
to be born	a se naşte	[a se 'naʃte]
delivery, labor	naştere (f)	['naʃtere]
to deliver (~ a baby)	a naşte	[a 'naʃte]
abortion	avort (n)	[a'vort]
breathing, respiration	respiraţie (f)	[respi'ratsie]
in-breath (inhalation)	inspiraţie (f)	[inspi'ratsie]

out-breath (exhalation)	**expirație** (f)	[ekspi'ratsie]
to exhale (breathe out)	**a expira**	[a ekspi'ra]
to inhale (vi)	**a inspira**	[a inspi'ra]
disabled person	**invalid** (m)	[inva'lid]
cripple	**infirm** (m)	[in'firm]
drug addict	**narcoman** (m)	[narko'man]
deaf (adj)	**surd**	[surd]
mute (adj)	**mut**	[mut]
deaf mute (adj)	**surdo-mut**	[surdo'mut]
mad, insane (adj)	**nebun**	[ne'bun]
madman	**nebun** (m)	[ne'bun]
(demented person)		
madwoman	**nebună** (f)	[ne'bunə]
to go insane	**a înnebuni**	[a innebu'ni]
gene	**genă** (f)	['dʒenə]
immunity	**imunitate** (f)	[imuni'tate]
hereditary (adj)	**ereditar**	[eredi'tar]
congenital (adj)	**congenital**	[kondʒeni'tal]
virus	**virus** (m)	['virus]
microbe	**microb** (m)	[mi'krob]
bacterium	**bacterie** (f)	[bak'terie]
infection	**infecție** (f)	[in'fektsie]

66. Symptoms. Treatments. Part 3

hospital	**spital** (n)	[spi'tal]
patient	**pacient** (m)	[patʃi'ent]
diagnosis	**diagnostic** (n)	[diag'nostik]
cure	**tratament** (n)	[trata'ment]
to get treatment	**a urma tratament**	[a ur'ma trata'ment]
to treat (~ a patient)	**a trata**	[a tra'ta]
to nurse (look after)	**a îngriji**	[a ingri'ʒi]
care (nursing ~)	**îngrijire** (f)	[ingri'ʒire]
operation, surgery	**operație** (f)	[ope'ratsie]
to bandage (head, limb)	**a pansa**	[a pan'sa]
bandaging	**pansare** (f)	[pan'sare]
vaccination	**vaccin** (n)	[vak'tʃin]
to vaccinate (vt)	**a vaccina**	[a vaktʃi'na]
injection, shot	**injecție** (f)	[in'ʒektsie]
to give an injection	**a face injecție**	[a 'fatʃe in'ʒektsie]
amputation	**amputare** (f)	[ampu'tare]
to amputate (vt)	**a amputa**	[a ampu'ta]

coma	comă (f)	['komə]
to be in a coma	a fi în comă	[a fi ɨn 'komə]
intensive care	reanimare (f)	[reani'mare]
to recover (~ from flu)	a se vindeca	[a se vinde'ka]
condition (patient's ~)	stare (f)	['stare]
consciousness	conştiinţă (f)	[konʃti'intsə]
memory (faculty)	memorie (f)	[me'morie]
to pull out (tooth)	a extrage	[a eks'tradʒe]
filling	plombă (f)	['plombə]
to fill (a tooth)	a plomba	[a plom'ba]
hypnosis	hipnoză (f)	[hip'nozə]
to hypnotize (vt)	a hipnotiza	[a hipnoti'za]

67. Medicine. Drugs. Accessories

medicine, drug	medicament (n)	[medika'ment]
remedy	remediu (n)	[re'medju]
to prescribe (vt)	a prescrie	[a pre'skrie]
prescription	reţetă (f)	[re'tsetə]
tablet, pill	pastilă (f)	[pas'tilə]
ointment	unguent (n)	[ungu'ent]
ampule	fiolă (f)	[fi'olə]
mixture, solution	mixtură (f)	[miks'turə]
syrup	sirop (n)	[si'rop]
capsule	pilulă (f)	[pi'lulə]
powder	praf (n)	[praf]
gauze bandage	bandaj (n)	[ban'daʒ]
cotton wool	vată (f)	['vatə]
iodine	iod (n)	[jod]
Band-Aid	leucoplast (n)	[leuko'plast]
eyedropper	pipetă (f)	[pi'petə]
thermometer	termometru (n)	[termo'metru]
syringe	seringă (f)	[se'ringə]
wheelchair	cărucior (n) pentru invalizi	[kəru'tʃior 'pentru inva'lizʲ]
crutches	cârje (f pl)	['kɨrʒe]
painkiller	anestezic (n)	[anes'tezik]
laxative	laxativ (n)	[laksa'tiv]
spirits (ethanol)	spirt (n)	[spirt]
medicinal herbs	plante (f pl) medicinale	['plante meditʃi'nale]
herbal (~ tea)	din plante medicinale	[din 'plante meditʃi'nale]

APARTMENT

T&P Books Publishing

68. Apartment

apartment	**apartament** (n)	[aparta'ment]
room	**cameră** (f)	['kamerə]
bedroom	**dormitor** (n)	[dormi'tor]
dining room	**sufragerie** (f)	[sufraʤe'rie]
living room	**salon** (n)	[sa'lon]
study (home office)	**cabinet** (n)	[kabi'net]
entry room	**antreu** (n)	[an'treu]
bathroom (room with a bath or shower)	**baie** (f)	['bae]
half bath	**toaletă** (f)	[toa'letə]
ceiling	**pod** (n)	[pod]
floor	**podea** (f)	[po'dʲa]
corner	**colţ** (n)	[kolts]

69. Furniture. Interior

furniture	**mobilă** (f)	['mobilə]
table	**masă** (f)	['masə]
chair	**scaun** (n)	['skaun]
bed	**pat** (n)	[pat]
couch, sofa	**divan** (n)	[di'van]
armchair	**fotoliu** (n)	[fo'tolju]
bookcase	**dulap** (n) **de cărţi**	[du'lap de kərts]
shelf	**raft** (n)	[raft]
wardrobe	**dulap** (n) **de haine**	[du'lap de 'hajne]
coat rack (wall-mounted ~)	**cuier** (n) **perete**	[ku'jer pe'rete]
coat stand	**cuier** (n) **pom**	[ku'jer pom]
bureau, dresser	**comodă** (f)	[ko'modə]
coffee table	**măsuţă** (f)	[mə'sutsə]
mirror	**oglindă** (f)	[og'lində]
carpet	**covor** (n)	[ko'vor]
rug, small carpet	**carpetă** (f)	[kar'petə]
fireplace	**şemineu** (n)	[ʃemi'neu]
candle	**lumânare** (f)	[lumʲ'nare]
candlestick	**sfeşnic** (n)	['sfeʃnik]

drapes	**draperii** (f pl)	[drape'rij]
wallpaper	**tapet** (n)	[ta'pet]
blinds (jalousie)	**jaluzele** (f pl)	[ʒalu'zele]
table lamp	**lampă** (f) **de birou**	['lampə de bi'rou]
wall lamp (sconce)	**lampă** (f)	['lampə]
floor lamp	**lampă** (f) **cu picior**	['lampə ku pi'ʧior]
chandelier	**lustră** (f)	['lustrə]
leg (of chair, table)	**picior** (n)	[pi'ʧior]
armrest	**braţ** (n) **la fotoliu**	['brats la fo'tolju]
back (backrest)	**spătar** (n)	[spə'tar]
drawer	**sertar** (n)	[ser'tar]

70. Bedding

bedclothes	**lenjerie** (f)	[lenʒe'rie]
pillow	**pernă** (f)	['pernə]
pillowcase	**faţă** (f) **de pernă**	['fatsə de 'pernə]
duvet, comforter	**plapumă** (f)	['plapumə]
sheet	**cearşaf** (n)	[ʧar'ʃaf]
bedspread	**pătură** (f)	[pəturə]

71. Kitchen

kitchen	**bucătărie** (f)	[bukətə'rie]
gas	**gaz** (n)	[gaz]
gas stove (range)	**aragaz** (n)	[ara'gaz]
electric stove	**plită** (f) **electrică**	['plitə e'lektrikə]
oven	**cuptor** (n)	[kup'tor]
microwave oven	**cuptor** (n) **cu microunde**	[kup'tor ku mikro'unde]
refrigerator	**frigider** (n)	[friʤi'der]
freezer	**congelator** (n)	[konʤela'tor]
dishwasher	**maşină** (f) **de spălat vase**	[ma'ʃinə de spə'lat 'vase]
meat grinder	**maşină** (f) **de tocat carne**	[ma'ʃinə de to'kat 'karne]
juicer	**storcător** (n)	[storkə'tor]
toaster	**prăjitor** (n) **de pâine**	[prəʒi'tor de 'pɨne]
mixer	**mixer** (n)	['mikser]
coffee machine	**fierbător** (n) **de cafea**	[fierbə'tor de ka'fa]
coffee pot	**ibric** (n)	[i'brik]
coffee grinder	**râşniţă** (f) **de cafea**	['riʃnitsə de ka'fa]
kettle	**ceainic** (n)	['ʧajnik]
teapot	**ceainic** (n)	['ʧajnik]
lid	**capac** (n)	[ka'pak]

tea strainer	strecurătoare (f)	[strekurəto'are]
spoon	lingură (f)	['lingurə]
teaspoon	linguriță (f) de ceai	[lingu'ritsə de tʃaj]
soup spoon	lingură (f)	['lingurə]
fork	furculiță (f)	[furku'litsə]
knife	cuțit (n)	[ku'tsit]

tableware (dishes)	vase (n pl)	['vase]
plate (dinner ~)	farfurie (f)	[farfu'rie]
saucer	farfurioară (f)	[farfurio'arə]

shot glass	păhărel (n)	[pəhə'rel]
glass (tumbler)	pahar (n)	[pa'har]
cup	ceașcă (f)	['tʃaʃkə]

sugar bowl	zaharniță (f)	[za'harnitsə]
salt shaker	solniță (f)	['solnitsə]
pepper shaker	piperniță (f)	[pi'pernitsə]
butter dish	untieră (f)	[un'tjerə]

stock pot (soup pot)	cratiță (f)	['kratitsə]
frying pan (skillet)	tigaie (f)	[ti'gae]
ladle	polonic (n)	[polo'nik]
colander	strecurătoare (f)	[strekurəto'are]
tray (serving ~)	tavă (f)	['tavə]

bottle	sticlă (f)	['stiklə]
jar (glass)	borcan (n)	[bor'kan]
can	cutie (f)	[ku'tie]

bottle opener	deschizător (n) de sticle	[deskizə'tor de 'stikle]
can opener	deschizător (n) de conserve	[deskizə'tor de kon'serve]
corkscrew	tirbușon (n)	[tirbu'ʃon]
filter	filtru (n)	['filtru]
to filter (vt)	a filtra	[a fil'tra]

| trash, garbage (food waste, etc.) | gunoi (n) | [gu'noj] |
| trash can (kitchen ~) | coș (n) de gunoi | [koʃ de gu'noj] |

72. Bathroom

bathroom	baie (f)	['bae]
water	apă (f)	['apə]
faucet	robinet (n)	[robi'net]
hot water	apă (f) fierbinte	['apə fjer'binte]
cold water	apă (f) rece	['apə 'retʃe]
toothpaste	pastă (f) de dinți	['pastə de dintsʲ]
to brush one's teeth	a se spăla pe dinți	[a se spə'la pe dintsʲ]

toothbrush	**periuță** (f) **de dinți**	[peri'ufsə de dints']
to shave (vi)	**a se bărbieri**	[a se bərbie'ri]
shaving foam	**spumă** (f) **de ras**	['spumə de 'ras]
razor	**brici** (n)	['britʃi]
to wash (one's hands, etc.)	**a spăla**	[a spə'la]
to take a bath	**a se spăla**	[a se spə'la]
shower	**duş** (n)	[duʃ]
to take a shower	**a face duş**	[a 'fatʃe duʃ]
bathtub	**cadă** (f)	['kadə]
toilet (toilet bowl)	**closet** (n)	[klo'set]
sink (washbasin)	**chiuvetă** (f)	[kju'vetə]
soap	**săpun** (n)	[sə'pun]
soap dish	**săpunieră** (f)	[səpu'njerə]
sponge	**burete** (n)	[bu'rete]
shampoo	**şampon** (n)	[ʃam'pon]
towel	**prosop** (n)	[pro'sop]
bathrobe	**halat** (n)	[ha'lat]
laundry (laundering)	**spălat** (n)	[spə'lat]
washing machine	**maşină** (f) **de spălat**	[ma'ʃinə de spə'lat]
to do the laundry	**a spăla haine**	[a spə'la 'hajne]
laundry detergent	**detergent** (n)	[deter'dʒent]

73. Household appliances

TV set	**televizor** (n)	[televi'zor]
tape recorder	**casetofon** (n)	[kaseto'fon]
VCR (video recorder)	**videomagnetofon** (n)	[videomagneto'fon]
radio	**aparat** (n) **de radio**	[apa'rat de 'radio]
player (CD, MP3, etc.)	**CD player** (n)	[si'di 'pleer]
video projector	**proiector** (n) **video**	[proek'tor 'video]
home movie theater	**sistem** (n) **home cinema**	[sis'tem 'houm 'sinema]
DVD player	**DVD-player** (n)	[divi'di 'pleer]
amplifier	**amplificator** (n)	[amplifi'kator]
video game console	**consolă** (f) **de jocuri**	[kon'solə de 'ʒokur']
video camera	**cameră** (f) **video**	['kamerə 'video]
camera (photo)	**aparat** (n) **foto**	[apa'rat 'foto]
digital camera	**aparat** (n) **foto digital**	[apa'rat 'foto didʒi'tal]
vacuum cleaner	**aspirator** (n)	[aspira'tor]
iron (e.g., steam ~)	**fier** (n) **de călcat**	[fier de kəl'kat]
ironing board	**masă** (f) **de călcat**	['masə de kəl'kat]
telephone	**telefon** (n)	[tele'fon]
cell phone	**telefon** (n) **mobil**	[tele'fon mo'bil]

| typewriter | **maşină** (f) **de scris** | [ma'ʃinə de skris] |
| sewing machine | **maşină** (f) **de cusut** | [ma'ʃine de ku'sut] |

microphone	**microfon** (n)	[mikro'fon]
headphones	**căşti** (f pl)	[kəʃtʲ]
remote control (TV)	**telecomandă** (f)	[teleko'mandə]

CD, compact disc	**CD** (n)	[si'di]
cassette, tape	**casetă** (f)	[ka'setə]
vinyl record	**placă** (f)	['plakə]

THE EARTH. WEATHER

T&P Books Publishing

space	**cosmos** (n)	['kosmos]
space (as adj)	**cosmic**	['kosmik]
outer space	**spaţiu** (n) **cosmic**	['spatsju 'kosmik]
world	**lume** (f)	['lume]
universe	**univers** (n)	[uni'vers]
galaxy	**galaxie** (f)	[galak'sie]
star	**stea** (f)	[st'a]
constellation	**constelaţie** (f)	[konste'latsie]
planet	**planetă** (f)	[pla'netə]
satellite	**satelit** (m)	[sate'lit]
meteorite	**meteorit** (m)	[meteo'rit]
comet	**cometă** (f)	[ko'metə]
asteroid	**asteroid** (m)	[astero'id]
orbit	**orbită** (f)	[or'bitə]
to revolve	**a se roti**	[a se ro'ti]
(~ around the Earth)		
atmosphere	**atmosferă** (f)	[atmos'ferə]
the Sun	**soare** (n)	[so'are]
solar system	**sistem** (n) **solar**	[sis'tem so'lar]
solar eclipse	**eclipsă** (f) **de soare**	[ek'lipse de so'are]
the Earth	**Pământ** (n)	[pə'mint]
the Moon	**Lună** (f)	['lunə]
Mars	**Marte** (m)	['marte]
Venus	**Venus** (f)	['venus]
Jupiter	**Jupiter** (m)	['ʒupiter]
Saturn	**Saturn** (m)	[sa'turn]
Mercury	**Mercur** (m)	[mer'kur]
Uranus	**Uranus** (m)	[u'ranus]
Neptune	**Neptun** (m)	[nep'tun]
Pluto	**Pluto** (m)	['pluto]
Milky Way	**Calea** (f) **Lactee**	['kal'a lak'tee]
Great Bear (Ursa Major)	**Ursa** (f) **mare**	['ursa 'mare]
North Star	**Steaua** (f) **polară**	['st'awa po'larə]
Martian	**marţian** (m)	[martsi'an]
extraterrestrial (n)	**extraterestru** (m)	[ekstrate'restru]

alien	extraterestru (m)	[ekstrate'restru]
flying saucer	farfurie (f) zburătoare	[farfu'rie zburəto'are]
spaceship	navă (f) spaţială	['navə spatsi'alə]
space station	staţie (f) orbitală	['statsie orbi'talə]
blast-off	start (n)	[start]
engine	motor (n)	[mo'tor]
nozzle	ajutaj (n)	[aʒu'taʒ]
fuel	combustibil (m)	[kombus'tibil]
cockpit, flight deck	cabină (f)	[ka'binə]
antenna	antenă (f)	[an'tenə]
porthole	hublou (n)	[hu'blou]
solar panel	baterie (f) solară	[bate'rie so'larə]
spacesuit	scafandru (m)	[ska'fandru]
weightlessness	imponderabilitate (f)	[imponderabili'tate]
oxygen	oxigen (n)	[oksi'dʒen]
docking (in space)	unire (f)	[u'nire]
to dock (vi, vt)	a uni	[a u'ni]
observatory	observator (n) astronomic	[observa'tor astro'nomik]
telescope	telescop (n)	[tele'skop]
to observe (vt)	a observa	[a obser'va]
to explore (vt)	a cerceta	[a t͡ʃert͡ʃe'ta]

75. The Earth

the Earth	Pământ (n)	[pə'mɨnt]
the globe (the Earth)	globul (n) pământesc	['globul pəmɨn'tesk]
planet	planetă (f)	[pla'netə]
atmosphere	atmosferă (f)	[atmos'ferə]
geography	geografie (f)	[dʒeogra'fie]
nature	natură (f)	[na'turə]
globe (table ~)	glob (n)	[glob]
map	hartă (f)	['hartə]
atlas	atlas (n)	[at'las]
Europe	Europa (f)	[eu'ropa]
Asia	Asia (f)	['asia]
Africa	Africa (f)	['afrika]
Australia	Australia (f)	[au'stralia]
America	America (f)	[a'merika]
North America	America (f) de Nord	[a'merika de nord]

South America	America (f) de Sud	[a'merika de sud]
Antarctica	Antarctida (f)	[ạntark'tida]
the Arctic	Arctica (f)	['arktika]

76. Cardinal directions

north	nord (n)	[nord]
to the north	la nord	[la nord]
in the north	la nord	[la nord]
northern (adj)	de nord	[de nord]

south	sud (n)	[sud]
to the south	la sud	[la sud]
in the south	la sud	[la sud]
southern (adj)	de sud	[de sud]

west	vest (n)	[vest]
to the west	la vest	[la vest]
in the west	la vest	[la vest]
western (adj)	de vest	[de vest]

east	est (n)	[est]
to the east	la est	[la est]
in the east	la est	[la est]
eastern (adj)	de est	[de est]

77. Sea. Ocean

sea	mare (f)	['mare]
ocean	ocean (n)	[otʃe'an]
gulf (bay)	golf (n)	[golf]
straits	strâmtoare (f)	[strịmto'are]

land (solid ground)	pământ (n)	[pə'mịnt]
continent (mainland)	continent (n)	[konti'nent]
island	insulă (f)	['insulə]
peninsula	peninsulă (f)	[pe'ninsulə]
archipelago	arhipelag (n)	[arhipe'lag]

bay, cove	golf (n)	[golf]
harbor	port (n)	[port]
lagoon	lagună (f)	[la'gunə]
cape	cap (n)	[kap]

atoll	atol (m)	[a'tol]
reef	recif (m)	[re'tʃif]
coral	coral (m)	[ko'ral]
coral reef	recif (m) de corali	[re'tʃif de ko'ralʲ]

deep (adj)	**adânc**	[a'dɨnk]
depth (deep water)	**adâncime** (f)	[adɨn'tʃime]
abyss	**abis** (n)	[a'bis]
trench (e.g., Mariana ~)	**groapă** (f)	[gro'apə]
current (Ocean ~)	**curent** (n)	[ku'rent]
to surround (bathe)	**a spăla**	[a spə'la]
shore	**mal** (n)	[mal]
coast	**litoral** (n)	[lito'ral]
flow (flood tide)	**flux** (n)	[fluks]
ebb (ebb tide)	**reflux** (n)	[re'fluks]
shoal	**banc** (n) **de nisip**	[bank de ni'sip]
bottom (~ of the sea)	**fund** (n)	[fund]
wave	**val** (n)	[val]
crest (~ of a wave)	**creasta** (f) **valului**	['krʲasta 'valuluj]
spume (sea foam)	**spumă** (f)	['spumə]
storm (sea storm)	**furtună** (f)	[fur'tunə]
hurricane	**uragan** (m)	[ura'gan]
tsunami	**tsunami** (n)	[tsu'nami]
calm (dead ~)	**timp** (n) **calm**	[timp kalm]
quiet, calm (adj)	**liniştit**	[liniʃ'tit]
pole	**pol** (n)	[pol]
polar (adj)	**polar**	[po'lar]
latitude	**longitudine** (f)	[londʒi'tudine]
longitude	**latitudine** (f)	[lati'tudine]
parallel	**paralelă** (f)	[para'lelə]
equator	**ecuator** (n)	[ekua'tor]
sky	**cer** (n)	[tʃer]
horizon	**orizont** (n)	[ori'zont]
air	**aer** (n)	['aer]
lighthouse	**far** (n)	[far]
to dive (vi)	**a se scufunda**	[a se skufun'da]
to sink (ab. boat)	**a se duce la fund**	[a se dutʃe lʲa fund]
treasures	**comoară** (f)	[komo'arə]

78. Seas' and Oceans' names

Atlantic Ocean	**Oceanul** (n) **Atlantic**	[otʃə'anul at'lantik]
Indian Ocean	**Oceanul** (n) **Indian**	[otʃə'anul indi'an]
Pacific Ocean	**Oceanul** (n) **Pacific**	[otʃə'anul pa'tʃifik]
Arctic Ocean	**Oceanul** (n) **Îngheţat de Nord**	[otʃə'anul inge'tsat de nord]

Black Sea	Marea (f) Neagră	['mar'a 'n'agrə]
Red Sea	Marea (f) Roşie	['mar'a 'roʃie]
Yellow Sea	Marea (f) Galbenă	['mar'a 'galbenə]
White Sea	Marea (f) Albă	['mar'a 'albə]

Caspian Sea	Marea (f) Caspică	['mar'a 'kaspikə]
Dead Sea	Marea (f) Moartă	['mar'a mo'artə]
Mediterranean Sea	Marea (f) Mediterană	['mar'a medite'ranə]

| Aegean Sea | Marea (f) Egee | ['mar'a e'ʤee] |
| Adriatic Sea | Marea (f) Adriatică | ['mar'a adri'atikə] |

Arabian Sea	Marea (f) Arabiei	['mar'a a'rabiej]
Sea of Japan	Marea (f) Japoneză	['mar'a ʒapo'nezə]
Bering Sea	Marea (f) Bering	['mar'a 'bering]
South China Sea	Marea (f) Chinei de Sud	['mar'a 'kinej de sud]

Coral Sea	Marea (f) Coral	['mar'a ko'ral]
Tasman Sea	Marea (f) Tasmaniei	['mar'a tas'maniej]
Caribbean Sea	Marea (f) Caraibelor	['mar'a kara'ibelor]

| Barents Sea | Marea (f) Barents | ['mar'a ba'rents] |
| Kara Sea | Marea (f) Kara | ['mar'a 'kara] |

North Sea	Marea (f) Nordului	['mar'a 'norduluj]
Baltic Sea	Marea (f) Baltică	['mar'a 'baltikə]
Norwegian Sea	Marea (f) Norvegiei	['mar'a nor'veʤiej]

79. Mountains

mountain	munte (m)	['munte]
mountain range	lanţ (n) muntos	[lants mun'tos]
mountain ridge	lanţ (n) de munţi	[lants de munts]

summit, top	vârf (n)	[virf]
peak	culme (f)	['kulmə]
foot (~ of the mountain)	poale (f pl)	[po'ale]
slope (mountainside)	pantă (f)	['pantə]

volcano	vulcan (n)	[vul'kan]
active volcano	vulcan (n) activ	[vul'kan ak'tiv]
dormant volcano	vulcan (n) stins	[vul'kan stins]

eruption	erupţie (f)	[e'ruptsie]
crater	crater (n)	['krater]
magma	magmă (f)	['magmə]
lava	lavă (f)	['lavə]
molten (~ lava)	încins	[in'tʃins]
canyon	canion (n)	[kani'on]
gorge	defileu (n)	[defi'leu]

crevice	pas (n)	[pas]
abyss (chasm)	prăpastie (f)	[prə'pastie]
pass, col	trecătoare (f)	[trekəto'are]
plateau	podiş (n)	[po'diʃ]
cliff	stâncă (f)	['stɨnkə]
hill	deal (n)	['dʲal]
glacier	gheţar (m)	[ge'ʦar]
waterfall	cascadă (f)	[kas'kadə]
geyser	gheizer (m)	['gejzer]
lake	lac (n)	[lak]
plain	şes (n)	[ʃəs]
landscape	peisaj (n)	[pej'saʒ]
echo	ecou (n)	[e'kou]
alpinist	alpinist (m)	[alpi'nist]
rock climber	căţărător (m)	[keʦərə'tor]
to conquer (in climbing)	a cuceri	[a kuʧe'ri]
climb (an easy ~)	ascensiune (f)	[asʧensi'une]

80. Mountains names

The Alps	Alpi (m pl)	['alpʲ]
Mont Blanc	Mont Blanc (m)	[mon 'blan]
The Pyrenees	Pirinei (m)	[piri'nej]
The Carpathians	Carpaţi (m pl)	[kar'patsʲ]
The Ural Mountains	Munţii (m pl) Ural	['munʦij u'ral]
The Caucasus Mountains	Caucaz (m)	[kau'kaz]
Mount Elbrus	Elbrus (m)	['elbrus]
The Altai Mountains	Altai (m)	[al'taj]
The Tian Shan	Tian-Şan (m)	['tjan 'ʃan]
The Pamir Mountains	Pamir (m)	[pa'mir]
The Himalayas	Himalaya	[hima'laja]
Mount Everest	Everest (m)	[eve'rest]
The Andes	Anzi	['anzʲ]
Mount Kilimanjaro	Kilimanjaro (m)	[kiliman'ʒaro]

81. Rivers

river	râu (n)	['riu]
spring (natural source)	izvor (n)	[iz'vor]
riverbed (river channel)	matcă (f)	['matkə]
basin (river valley)	bazin (n)	[ba'zin]

to flow into …	a se vărsa	[a se vər'sa]
tributary	afluent (m)	[aflu'ent]
bank (of river)	mal (n)	[mal]

current (stream)	curs (n)	[kurs]
downstream (adv)	în josul apei	[ɨn 'ʒosul 'apej]
upstream (adv)	în susul apei	[ɨn 'susul 'apej]

inundation	inundație (f)	[inun'datsie]
flooding	revărsare (f) a apelor	[revər'sare a 'apelor]
to overflow (vi)	a se revărsa	[a se revər'sa]
to flood (vt)	a inunda	[a inun'da]

| shallow (shoal) | banc (n) de nisip | [bank de ni'sip] |
| rapids | prag (n) | [prag] |

dam	baraj (n)	[ba'raʒ]
canal	canal (n)	[ka'nal]
reservoir (artificial lake)	bazin (n)	[ba'zin]
sluice, lock	ecluză (f)	[e'kluzə]

water body (pond, etc.)	bazin (n)	[ba'zin]
swamp (marshland)	mlaştină (f)	['mlaʃtine]
bog, marsh	mlaştină (f), smârc (n)	['mlaʃtine], [smɨrk]
whirlpool	vârtej (n) de apă	[vɨr'teʒ de 'apə]

stream (brook)	pârâu (n)	[pɨ'rɨu]
drinking (ab. water)	potabil	[po'tabil]
fresh (~ water)	nesărat	[nese'rat]

| ice | gheață (f) | ['gʲatsə] |
| to freeze over (ab. river, etc.) | a îngheța | [a ɨnge'tsa] |

82. Rivers' names

| Seine | Sena (f) | ['sena] |
| Loire | Loara (f) | [lo'ara] |

Thames	Tamisa (f)	[ta'misa]
Rhine	Rin (m)	[rin]
Danube	Dunăre (f)	['dunere]

Volga	Volga (f)	['volga]
Don	Don (m)	[don]
Lena	Lena (f)	['lena]

Yellow River	Huang He (m)	[huan 'he]
Yangtze	Yangtze (m)	[jants'zɨ]
Mekong	Mekong (m)	[me'kong]

Ganges	**Gang** (m)	[gang]
Nile River	**Nil** (m)	[nil]
Congo River	**Congo** (m)	['kongo]
Okavango River	**Okavango** (m)	[oka'vango]
Zambezi River	**Zambezi** (m)	[zam'bezi]
Limpopo River	**Limpopo** (m)	[limpo'po]
Mississippi River	**Mississippi** (m)	[misi'sipi]

83. Forest

| forest, wood | **pădure** (f) | [pə'dure] |
| forest (as adj) | **de pădure** | [de pə'dure] |

thick forest	**desiş** (n)	[de'siʃ]
grove	**pădurice** (f)	[pədu'ritʃe]
forest clearing	**poiană** (f)	[po'janə]

| thicket | **tufiş** (n) | [tu'fiʃ] |
| scrubland | **arbust** (m) | [ar'bust] |

| footpath (troddenpath) | **cărare** (f) | [kə'rare] |
| gully | **râpă** (f) | ['ripə] |

tree	**copac** (m)	[ko'pak]
leaf	**frunză** (f)	['frunzə]
leaves (foliage)	**frunziş** (n)	[frun'ziʃ]

fall of leaves	**cădere** (f) **a frunzelor**	[kə'dere a 'frunzelor]
to fall (ab. leaves)	**a cădea**	[a kə'dʲa]
top (of the tree)	**vârf** (n)	[virf]

branch	**ramură** (f)	['ramurə]
bough	**creangă** (f)	['krʲangə]
bud (on shrub, tree)	**mugur** (m)	['mugur]
needle (of pine tree)	**ac** (n)	[ak]
pine cone	**con** (n)	[kon]

tree hollow	**scorbură** (f)	['skorburə]
nest	**cuib** (n)	[kujb]
burrow (animal hole)	**vizuină** (f)	[vizu'inə]

trunk	**trunchi** (n)	[trunkʲ]
root	**rădăcină** (f)	[rədə'tʃinə]
bark	**scoarţă** (f)	[sko'artsə]
moss	**muşchi** (m)	[muʃkʲ]

to uproot (remove trees or tree stumps)	**a defrişa**	[a defri'ʃa]
to chop down	**a tăia**	[a tə'ja]
to deforest (vt)	**a doborî**	[a dobo'ri]

tree stump	buturugă (f)	[butu'rugə]
campfire	foc (n)	[fok]
forest fire	incendiu (n)	[in'tʃendju]
to extinguish (vt)	a stinge	[a 'stindʒe]

forest ranger	pădurar (m)	[pədu'rar]
protection	protecţie (f)	[pro'tektsie]
to protect (~ nature)	a ocroti	[a okro'ti]
poacher	braconier (m)	[brako'njer]
steel trap	capcană (f)	[kap'kanə]

| to gather, to pick (vt) | a strânge | [a 'strɨndʒe] |
| to lose one's way | a se rătăci | [a se rətə'tʃi] |

84. Natural resources

natural resources	resurse (f pl) naturale	[re'surse natu'rale]
minerals	bogăţii (f pl) minerale	[boge'tsij mine'rale]
deposits	depozite (n pl)	[de'pozite]
field (e.g., oilfield)	zăcământ (n)	[zəkə'mɨnt]

to mine (extract)	a extrage	[a eks'tradʒe]
mining (extraction)	obţinere (f)	[ob'tsinere]
ore	minereu (n)	[mine'reu]
mine (e.g., for coal)	mină (f)	['minə]
shaft (mine ~)	puţ (n)	['puts]
miner	miner (m)	[mi'ner]

| gas (natural ~) | gaz (n) | [gaz] |
| gas pipeline | conductă (f) de gaze | [kon'duktə de 'gaze] |

oil (petroleum)	petrol (n)	[pe'trol]
oil pipeline	conductă (f) de petrol	[kon'duktə de pe'trol]
oil well	sondă (f) de ţiţei (n)	['sonde de tsi'tsej]
derrick (tower)	turlă (f) de foraj	['turle de fo'raʒ]
tanker	tanc (n) petrolier	['tank petro'ljer]

sand	nisip (n)	[ni'sip]
limestone	calcar (n)	[kal'kar]
gravel	pietriş (n)	[pe'triʃ]
peat	turbă (f)	['turbə]
clay	argilă (f)	[ar'dʒilə]
coal	cărbune (m)	[kər'bune]

iron (ore)	fier (m)	[fier]
gold	aur (n)	['aur]
silver	argint (n)	[ar'dʒint]
nickel	nichel (n)	['nikel]
copper	cupru (n)	['kupru]
zinc	zinc (n)	[zink]

manganese	mangan (n)	[man'gan]
mercury	mercur (n)	[mer'kur]
lead	plumb (n)	[plumb]

mineral	mineral (n)	[mine'ral]
crystal	cristal (n)	[kris'tal]
marble	marmură (f)	['marmurə]
uranium	uraniu (n)	[u'ranju]

85. Weather

weather	timp (n)	[timp]
weather forecast	prognoză (f) meteo	[prog'nozə 'meteo]
temperature	temperatură (f)	[tempera'turə]
thermometer	termometru (n)	[termo'metru]
barometer	barometru (n)	[baro'metru]

humid (adj)	umed	['umed]
humidity	umiditate (f)	[umidi'tate]
heat (extreme ~)	caniculă (f)	[ka'nikulə]
hot (torrid)	fierbinte	[fier'binte]
it's hot	e foarte cald	[e fo'arte kald]

| it's warm | e cald | [e kald] |
| warm (moderately hot) | cald | [kald] |

| it's cold | e frig | [e frig] |
| cold (adj) | rece | ['retʃe] |

sun	soare (n)	[so'are]
to shine (vi)	a străluci	[a strəlu'tʃi]
sunny (day)	însorit	[inso'rit]
to come up (vi)	a răsări	[a rəsə'ri]
to set (vi)	a apune	[a a'pune]

cloud	nor (m)	[nor]
cloudy (adj)	înnorat	[inno'rat]
rain cloud	nor (m)	[nor]
somber (gloomy)	mohorât	[moho'rit]

rain	ploaie (f)	[plo'ae]
it's raining	plouă	['plowə]
rainy (~ day, weather)	ploios	[plo'jos]
to drizzle (vi)	a bura	[a bu'ra]

pouring rain	ploaie (f) torenţială	[plo'ae toren'tsjale]
downpour	rupere (f) de nori	['rupere de 'nori]
heavy (e.g., ~ rain)	puternic	[pu'ternik]
puddle	băltoacă (f)	[belto'akə]
to get wet (in rain)	a se uda	[a se u'da]

fog (mist)	ceață (f)	['tʃatsə]
foggy	cețos	[tʃe'tsos]
snow	zăpadă (f)	[zə'padə]
it's snowing	ninge	['nindʒe]

86. Severe weather. Natural disasters

thunderstorm	furtună (f)	[fur'tunə]
lightning (~ strike)	fulger (n)	['fuldʒer]
to flash (vi)	a fulgera	[a fuldʒe'ra]
thunder	tunet (n)	['tunet]
to thunder (vi)	a tuna	[a tu'na]
it's thundering	tună	['tunə]
hail	grindină (f)	[grin'dinə]
it's hailing	plouă cu gheață	['plowə ku 'gⁱatsə]
to flood (vt)	a inunda	[a inun'da]
flood, inundation	inundație (f)	[inun'datsie]
earthquake	cutremur (n)	[ku'tremur]
tremor, shoke	zguduire (f)	[zgudu'ire]
epicenter	epicentru (m)	[epi'tʃentru]
eruption	erupție (f)	[e'ruptsie]
lava	lavă (f)	['lavə]
twister	vârtej (n)	[vɨr'teʒ]
tornado	tornadă (f)	[tor'nadə]
typhoon	taifun (n)	[taj'fun]
hurricane	uragan (m)	[ura'gan]
storm	furtună (f)	[fur'tunə]
tsunami	tsunami (n)	[tsu'nami]
cyclone	ciclon (m)	[tʃi'klon]
bad weather	vreme (f) rea	['vreme rⁱa]
fire (accident)	incendiu (n)	[in'tʃendju]
disaster	catastrofă (f)	[katas'trofə]
meteorite	meteorit (m)	[meteo'rit]
avalanche	avalanșă (f)	[ava'lanʃə]
snowslide	prăbușire (f)	[prəbu'ʃire]
blizzard	viscol (n)	['viskol]
snowstorm	viscol (n)	['viskol]

FAUNA

T&P Books Publishing

predator	**prădător** (n)	[prədə'tor]
tiger	**tigru** (m)	['tigru]
lion	**leu** (m)	['leu]
wolf	**lup** (m)	[lup]
fox	**vulpe** (f)	['vulpe]
jaguar	**jaguar** (m)	[ʒagu'ar]
leopard	**leopard** (m)	[leo'pard]
cheetah	**ghepard** (m)	[ge'pard]
black panther	**panteră** (f)	[pan'terə]
puma	**pumă** (f)	['pumə]
snow leopard	**ghepard** (m)	[ge'pard]
lynx	**râs** (m)	[ris]
coyote	**coiot** (m)	[ko'jot]
jackal	**şacal** (m)	[ʃa'kal]
hyena	**hienă** (f)	[hi'enə]

animal	**animal** (n)	[ani'mal]
beast (animal)	**animal** (n) **sălbatic**	[ani'mal səl'batik]
squirrel	**veveriţă** (f)	[veve'ritsə]
hedgehog	**arici** (m)	[a'ritʃi]
hare	**iepure** (m)	['jepure]
rabbit	**iepure** (m) **de casă**	['jepure de 'kasə]
badger	**bursuc** (m)	[bur'suk]
raccoon	**enot** (m)	[e'not]
hamster	**hârciog** (m)	[hir'tʃiog]
marmot	**marmotă** (f)	[mar'motə]
mole	**cârtiţă** (f)	['kirtitsə]
mouse	**şoarece** (m)	[ʃo'aretʃe]
rat	**şobolan** (m)	[ʃobo'lan]
bat	**liliac** (m)	[lili'ak]
ermine	**hermină** (f)	[her'minə]
sable	**samur** (m)	[sa'mur]
marten	**jder** (m)	[ʒder]

| weasel | nevăstuică (f) | [nevəs'tujkə] |
| mink | nurcă (f) | ['nurkə] |

| beaver | castor (m) | ['kastor] |
| otter | vidră (f) | ['vidrə] |

horse	cal (m)	[kal]
moose	elan (m)	[e'lan]
deer	cerb (m)	[ʧerb]
camel	cămilă (f)	[kə'milə]

bison	bizon (m)	[bi'zon]
wisent	zimbru (m)	['zimbru]
buffalo	bivol (m)	['bivol]

zebra	zebră (f)	['zebrə]
antelope	antilopă (f)	[anti'lopə]
roe deer	căprioară (f)	[kəprio'arə]
fallow deer	ciută (f)	['ʧiutə]
chamois	capră (f) neagră	['kaprə 'nʲagrə]
wild boar	mistreț (m)	[mis'trets]

whale	balenă (f)	[ba'lenə]
seal	focă (f)	['fokə]
walrus	morsă (f)	['morsə]
fur seal	urs (m) de mare	[urs de 'mare]
dolphin	delfin (m)	[del'fin]

bear	urs (m)	[urs]
polar bear	urs (m) polar	[urs po'lar]
panda	panda (m)	['panda]

monkey	maimuță (f)	[maj'mutsə]
chimpanzee	cimpanzeu (m)	[ʧimpan'zeu]
orangutan	urangutan (m)	[urangu'tan]
gorilla	gorilă (f)	[go'rilə]
macaque	macac (m)	[ma'kak]
gibbon	gibon (m)	[dʒi'bon]

| elephant | elefant (m) | [ele'fant] |
| rhinoceros | rinocer (m) | [rino'ʧer] |

| giraffe | girafă (f) | [dʒi'rafə] |
| hippopotamus | hipopotam (m) | [hipopo'tam] |

| kangaroo | cangur (m) | ['kangur] |
| koala (bear) | koala (f) | [ko'ala] |

mongoose	mangustă (f)	[man'gustə]
chinchilla	şinşilă (f)	[ʃin'ʃilə]
skunk	sconcs (m)	[skonks]
porcupine	porc (m) spinos	[pork spi'nos]

89. Domestic animals

cat	pisică (f)	[pi'sikə]
tomcat	motan (m)	[mo'tan]
dog	câine (m)	['kɨjnə]
horse	cal (m)	[kal]
stallion (male horse)	armăsar (m)	[armə'sar]
mare	iapă (f)	['japə]
cow	vacă (f)	['vakə]
bull	taur (m)	['taur]
ox	bou (m)	['bou]
sheep (ewe)	oaie (f)	[o'ae]
ram	berbec (m)	[ber'bek]
goat	capră (f)	['kaprə]
billy goat, he-goat	ţap (m)	[ʦap]
donkey	măgar (m)	[mə'gar]
mule	catâr (m)	[ka'tɨr]
pig, hog	porc (m)	[pork]
piglet	purcel (m)	[pur'ʧel]
rabbit	iepure (m) de casă	['jepure de 'kasə]
hen (chicken)	găină (f)	[gə'inə]
rooster	cocoş (m)	[ko'koʃ]
duck	raţă (f)	['raʦə]
drake	răţoi (m)	[rə'ʦoj]
goose	gâscă (f)	['gɨskə]
tom turkey, gobbler	curcan (m)	[kur'kan]
turkey (hen)	curcă (f)	['kurkə]
domestic animals	animale (n pl) domestice	[ani'male do'mestiʧe]
tame (e.g., ~ hamster)	domestic	[do'mestik]
to tame (vt)	a domestici	[a domesti'ʧi]
to breed (vt)	a creşte	[a 'kreʃte]
farm	fermă (f)	['fermə]
poultry	păsări (f pl) de curte	[pəsərʲ de 'kurte]
cattle	vite (f pl)	['vite]
herd (cattle)	turmă (f)	['turmə]
stable	grajd (n)	[graʒd]
pigpen	cocină (f) de porci	[ko'ʧinə de 'porʧi]
cowshed	grajd (n) pentru vaci	['graʒd 'pentru 'vaʧi]
rabbit hutch	cuşcă (f) pentru iepuri	['kuʃkə 'pentru 'epurʲ]
hen house	coteţ (n) de găini	[ko'teʦ de gə'inʲ]

90. Birds

bird	pasăre (f)	['pasəre]
pigeon	porumbel (m)	[porum'bel]
sparrow	vrabie (f)	['vrabie]
tit (great tit)	pițigoi (m)	[pitsi'goj]
magpie	coțofană (f)	[kotso'fanə]
raven	corb (m)	[korb]
crow	cioară (f)	[tʃio'arə]
jackdaw	stancă (f)	['stankə]
rook	cioară (f) de câmp	[tʃio'arə de 'kɨmp]
duck	rață (f)	['ratsə]
goose	gâscă (f)	['gɨskə]
pheasant	fazan (m)	[fa'zan]
eagle	acvilă (f)	['akvilə]
hawk	uliu (m)	['ulju]
falcon	şoim (m)	[ʃojm]
vulture	vultur (m)	['vultur]
condor (Andean ~)	condor (m)	[kon'dor]
swan	lebădă (f)	['lebədə]
crane	cocor (m)	[ko'kor]
stork	cocostârc (m)	[kokos'tɨrk]
parrot	papagal (m)	[papa'gal]
hummingbird	pasărea (f) colibri	['pasərʲa ko'libri]
peacock	păun (m)	[pə'un]
ostrich	struț (m)	[struts]
heron	stârc (m)	[stɨrk]
flamingo	flamingo (m)	[fla'mingo]
pelican	pelican (m)	[peli'kan]
nightingale	privighetoare (f)	[privigeto'are]
swallow	rândunică (f)	[rɨndu'nikə]
thrush	mierlă (f)	['merlə]
song thrush	sturz-cântător (m)	[sturz kɨntə'tor]
blackbird	mierlă (f) sură	['merlə 'surə]
swift	lăstun (m)	[ləs'tun]
lark	ciocârlie (f)	[tʃiokɨr'lie]
quail	prepeliță (f)	[prepe'litsə]
woodpecker	ciocănitoare (f)	[tʃiokənito'are]
cuckoo	cuc (m)	[kuk]
owl	bufniță (f)	['bufnitsə]
eagle owl	buha mare (f)	['buhə 'mare]

wood grouse	cocoş (m) de munte	[ko'koʃ de 'munte]
black grouse	cocoş (m) sălbatic	[ko'koʃ səlba'tik]
partridge	potârniche (f)	[potir'nike]

starling	graur (m)	['graur]
canary	canar (m)	[ka'nar]
hazel grouse	găinuşă de alun (f)	[gəi'nuʃə de a'lun]
chaffinch	cinteză (f)	[tʃin'tezə]
bullfinch	botgros (m)	[bot'gros]

seagull	pescăruş (m)	[peskə'ruʃ]
albatross	albatros (m)	[alba'tros]
penguin	pinguin (m)	[pigu'in]

91. Fish. Marine animals

bream	plătică (f)	[plə'tikə]
carp	crap (m)	[krap]
perch	biban (m)	[bi'ban]
catfish	somn (m)	[somn]
pike	ştiucă (f)	['ʃtjukə]

salmon	somon (m)	[so'mon]
sturgeon	nisetru (m)	[ni'setru]

herring	scrumbie (f)	[skrum'bie]
Atlantic salmon	somon (m)	[so'mon]
mackerel	macrou (n)	[ma'krou]
flatfish	cambulă (f)	[kam'bulə]

zander, pike perch	şalău (m)	[ʃa'ləu]
cod	batog (m)	[ba'tog]
tuna	ton (m)	[ton]
trout	păstrăv (m)	[pəs'trəv]

eel	ţipar (m)	[tsi'par]
electric ray	peşte-torpilă (m)	['peʃte tor'pilə]
moray eel	murenă (f)	[mu'renə]
piranha	piranha (f)	[pi'ranija]

shark	rechin (m)	[re'kin]
dolphin	delfin (m)	[del'fin]
whale	balenă (f)	[ba'lenə]

crab	crab (m)	[krab]
jellyfish	meduză (f)	[me'duzə]
octopus	caracatiţă (f)	[kara'katitsə]

starfish	stea de mare (f)	[st'a de 'mare]
sea urchin	arici de mare (m)	[a'ritʃi de 'mare]

seahorse	căluţ (m) de mare (f)	[ka'luts de 'mare]
oyster	stridie (f)	['stridie]
shrimp	crevetă (f)	[kre'vetə]
lobster	stacoj (m)	[sta'koʒ]
spiny lobster	langustă (f)	[lan'gustə]

92. Amphibians. Reptiles

| snake | şarpe (m) | ['ʃarpe] |
| venomous (snake) | veninos | [veni'nos] |

viper	viperă (f)	['viperə]
cobra	cobră (f)	['kobrə]
python	piton (m)	[pi'ton]
boa	şarpe (m) boa	['ʃarpe bo'a]

grass snake	şarpe (m) de casă	['ʃarpe de 'kasə]
rattle snake	şarpe (m) cu clopoţei	['ʃarpe ku klopo'tsej]
anaconda	anacondă (f)	[ana'kondə]

lizard	şopârlă (f)	[ʃo'pɨrlə]
iguana	iguană (f)	[igu'anə]
monitor lizard	şopârlă (f)	[ʃo'pɨrlə]
salamander	salamandră (f)	[sala'mandrə]
chameleon	cameleon (m)	[kamele'on]
scorpion	scorpion (m)	[skorpi'on]

turtle	broască (f) ţestoasă	[bro'askə tsesto'asə]
frog	broască (f)	[bro'askə]
toad	broască (f) râioasă	[bro'askə rɨjo'asə]
crocodile	crocodil (m)	[kroko'dil]

93. Insects

insect, bug	insectă (f)	[in'sektə]
butterfly	fluture (m)	['fluture]
ant	furnică (f)	[fur'nikə]
fly	muscă (f)	['muskə]
mosquito	ţânţar (m)	[tsɨn'tsar]
beetle	gândac (m)	[gɨn'dak]

wasp	viespe (f)	['vespe]
bee	albină (f)	[al'binə]
bumblebee	bondar (m)	[bon'dar]
gadfly (botfly)	tăun (m)	[tə'un]

| spider | păianjen (m) | [pə'janʒen] |
| spiderweb | pânză (f) de păianjen | ['pɨnzə de pə'janʒen] |

dragonfly	**libelulă** (f)	[libe'lulə]
grasshopper	**greier** (m)	['greer]
moth (night butterfly)	**fluture** (m)	['fluture]
cockroach	**gândac** (m)	[gɨn'dak]
tick	**căpuşă** (f)	[kə'puʃə]
flea	**purice** (m)	['puritʃe]
midge	**musculiţă** (f)	[musku'litsə]
locust	**lăcustă** (f)	[lə'kustə]
snail	**melc** (m)	[melk]
cricket	**greier** (m)	['greer]
lightning bug	**licurici** (m)	[liku'ritʃi]
ladybug	**buburuză** (f)	[bubu'ruzə]
cockchafer	**cărăbuş** (m)	[kərə'buʃ]
leech	**lipitoare** (f)	[lipito'are]
caterpillar	**omidă** (f)	[o'midə]
earthworm	**vierme** (m)	['verme]
larva	**larvă** (f)	['larvə]

FLORA

T&P Books Publishing

tree	copac (m)	[ko'pak]
deciduous (adj)	foios	[fo'jos]
coniferous (adj)	conifer	[koni'fere]
evergreen (adj)	veşnic verde	['veʃnik 'verde]

apple tree	măr (m)	[mər]
pear tree	păr (m)	[pər]
sweet cherry tree	cireş (m)	[tʃi'reʃ]
sour cherry tree	vişin (m)	['viʃin]
plum tree	prun (m)	[prun]

birch	mesteacăn (m)	[mes'tʲakən]
oak	stejar (m)	[ste'ʒar]
linden tree	tei (m)	[tej]
aspen	plop tremurător (m)	['plop tremurə'tor]
maple	arţar (m)	[ar'tsar]

spruce	brad (m)	[brad]
pine	pin (m)	[pin]
larch	zadă (f)	['zadə]

fir tree	brad (m) alb	['brad 'alb]
cedar	cedru (m)	['tʃedru]

poplar	plop (m)	[plop]
rowan	sorb (m)	[sorb]

willow	salcie (f)	['saltʃie]
alder	arin (m)	[a'rin]

beech	fag (m)	[fag]
elm	ulm (m)	[ulm]

ash (tree)	frasin (m)	['frasin]
chestnut	castan (m)	[kas'tan]

magnolia	magnolie (f)	[mag'nolie]
palm tree	palmier (m)	[palmi'er]
cypress	chiparos (m)	[kipa'ros]

mangrove	manglier (m)	[mangli'jer]
baobab	baobab (m)	[bao'bab]
eucalyptus	eucalipt (m)	[euka'lipt]
sequoia	secvoia (m)	[sek'voja]

95. Shrubs

bush	tufă (f)	['tufə]
shrub	arbust (m)	[ar'bust]
grapevine	viţă (f) de vie	['vitsə de 'vie]
vineyard	vie (f)	['vie]
raspberry bush	zmeură (f)	['zmeurə]
blackcurrant bush	coacăz (m) negru	[ko'akəz 'negru]
redcurrant bush	coacăz (m) roşu	[ko'akəz 'roʃu]
gooseberry bush	agriş (m)	[a'griʃ]
acacia	salcâm (m)	[sal'kɨm]
barberry	lemn (m) galben	['lemn 'galben]
jasmine	iasomie (f)	[jaso'mie]
juniper	ienupăr (m)	[je'nupər]
rosebush	tufă (f) de trandafir	['tufə de tranda'fir]
dog rose	măceş (m)	[mə'tʃeʃ]

96. Fruits. Berries

fruit	fruct (n)	[frukt]
fruits	fructe (n pl)	[frukte]
apple	măr (n)	[mər]
pear	pară (f)	['parə]
plum	prună (f)	['prunə]
strawberry (garden ~)	căpşună (f)	[kəp'ʃunə]
sour cherry	vişină (f)	['viʃinə]
sweet cherry	cireaşă (f)	[tʃi'rʲaʃə]
grape	struguri (m pl)	['strugurʲ]
raspberry	zmeură (f)	['zmeurə]
blackcurrant	coacăză (f) neagră	[ko'akəzə 'nʲagrə]
redcurrant	coacăză (f) roşie	[ko'akəzə 'roʃie]
gooseberry	agrişă (f)	[a'griʃə]
cranberry	răchiţele (f pl)	[rəki'tsele]
orange	portocală (f)	[porto'kalə]
mandarin	mandarină (f)	[manda'rinə]
pineapple	ananas (m)	[ana'nas]
banana	banană (f)	[ba'nanə]
date	curmală (f)	[kur'malə]
lemon	lămâie (f)	[lə'mɨe]
apricot	caisă (f)	[ka'isə]
peach	piersică (f)	['pjersikə]

| kiwi | kiwi (n) | ['kivi] |
| grapefruit | grepfrut (n) | ['grepfrut] |

berry	boabă (f)	[bo'abe]
berries	fructe (n pl) de pădure	['frukte de pe'dure]
cowberry	merişor (m)	[meri'ʃor]
wild strawberry	frag (m)	[frag]
bilberry	afină (f)	[a'fine]

97. Flowers. Plants

| flower | floare (f) | [flo'are] |
| bouquet (of flowers) | buchet (n) | [bu'ket] |

rose (flower)	trandafir (m)	[tranda'fir]
tulip	lalea (f)	[la'lʲa]
carnation	garoafă (f)	[garo'afe]
gladiolus	gladiolă (f)	[gladi'ole]

cornflower	albăstrea (f)	[albes'trʲa]
harebell	clopoţel (m)	[klopo'tsel]
dandelion	păpădie (f)	[pepe'die]
camomile	romaniţă (f)	[roma'nitse]

aloe	aloe (f)	[a'loe]
cactus	cactus (m)	['kaktus]
rubber plant, ficus	ficus (m)	['fikus]

lily	crin (m)	[krin]
geranium	muşcată (f)	[muʃ'kate]
hyacinth	zambilă (f)	[zam'bile]

mimosa	mimoză (f)	[mi'moze]
narcissus	narcisă (f)	[nar'tʃise]
nasturtium	condurul-doamnei (m)	[kon'durul do'amnej]

orchid	orhidee (f)	[orhi'dee]
peony	bujor (m)	[bu'ʒor]
violet	toporaş (m)	[topo'raʃ]

pansy	pansele (f)	[pan'sele]
forget-me-not	nu-mă-uita (f)	[nu me uj'ta]
daisy	margaretă (f)	[marga'rete]

poppy	mac (m)	[mak]
hemp	cânepă (f)	['kɨnepe]
mint	mentă (f)	['mente]

| lily of the valley | lăcrămioară (f) | [lekremjo'are] |
| snowdrop | ghiocel (m) | [gio'tʃel] |

nettle	urzică (f)	[ur'zikə]
sorrel	măcriş (m)	[mə'kriʃ]
water lily	nufăr (m)	['nufər]
fern	ferigă (f)	['ferigə]
lichen	lichen (m)	[li'ken]
conservatory (greenhouse)	seră (f)	['serə]
lawn	gazon (n)	[ga'zon]
flowerbed	strat (n) de flori	[strat de 'florʲ]
plant	plantă (f)	['plantə]
grass	iarbă (f)	['jarbə]
blade of grass	fir (n) de iarbă	[fir de 'jarbə]
leaf	frunză (f)	['frunzə]
petal	petală (f)	[pe'talə]
stem	tulpină (f)	[tul'pinə]
tuber	tubercul (m)	[tu'berkul]
young plant (shoot)	mugur (m)	['mugur]
thorn	ghimpe (m)	['gimpe]
to blossom (vi)	a înflori	[a ɨnflo'ri]
to fade, to wither	a se ofili	[a se ofe'li]
smell (odor)	miros (n)	[mi'ros]
to cut (flowers)	a tăia	[a tə'ja]
to pick (a flower)	a rupe	[a 'rupe]

98. Cereals, grains

grain	grăunţe (n pl)	[grə'untse]
cereal crops	cereale (f pl)	[tʃere'ale]
ear (of barley, etc.)	spic (n)	[spik]
wheat	grâu (n)	['grɨu]
rye	secară (f)	[se'karə]
oats	ovăz (n)	[ovəz]
millet	mei (m)	[mej]
barley	orz (n)	[orz]
corn	porumb (m)	[po'rumb]
rice	orez (n)	[o'rez]
buckwheat	hrişcă (f)	['hriʃkə]
pea plant	mazăre (f)	['mazere]
kidney bean	fasole (f)	[fa'sole]
soy	soia (f)	['soja]
lentil	linte (n)	['linte]
beans (pulse crops)	boabe (f pl)	[bo'abe]

COUNTRIES OF
THE WORLD

T&P Books Publishing

Afghanistan	**Afganistan** (n)	[afganis'tan]
Albania	**Albania** (f)	[al'banija]
Argentina	**Argentina** (f)	[arʒen'tina]
Armenia	**Armenia** (f)	[ar'menia]
Australia	**Australia** (f)	[au'stralia]
Austria	**Austria** (f)	[a'ustrija]
Azerbaijan	**Azerbaidjan** (m)	[azerbaj'dʒan]
The Bahamas	**Insulele** (f pl) **Bahamas**	['insulele ba'hamas]
Bangladesh	**Bangladeş** (m)	[bangla'deʃ]
Belarus	**Belarus** (f)	[bela'rus]
Belgium	**Belgia** (f)	['beldʒia]
Bolivia	**Bolivia** (f)	[bo'livia]
Bosnia and Herzegovina	**Bosnia şi Herţegovina** (f)	['bosnia ʃi herʦego'vina]
Brazil	**Brazilia** (f)	[bra'zilia]
Bulgaria	**Bulgaria** (f)	[bul'garia]
Cambodia	**Cambodgia** (f)	[kam'bodʒia]
Canada	**Canada** (f)	[ka'nada]
Chile	**Chile** (n)	['tʃile]
China	**China** (f)	['kina]
Colombia	**Columbia** (f)	[ko'lumbia]
Croatia	**Croaţia** (f)	[kro'aʦia]
Cuba	**Cuba** (f)	['kuba]
Cyprus	**Cipru** (n)	['tʃipru]
Czech Republic	**Cehia** (f)	['tʃehija]
Denmark	**Danemarca** (f)	[dane'marka]
Dominican Republic	**Republica** (f) **Dominicană**	[re'publika domini'kanə]
Ecuador	**Ecuador** (m)	[ekua'dor]
Egypt	**Egipt** (n)	[e'dʒipt]
England	**Anglia** (f)	['anglija]
Estonia	**Estonia** (f)	[es'tonia]
Finland	**Finlanda** (f)	[fin'landa]
France	**Franţa** (f)	['franʦa]
French Polynesia	**Polinezia** (f)	[poli'nezia]
Georgia	**Georgia** (f)	['dʒordʒia]
Germany	**Germania** (f)	[dʒer'manija]
Ghana	**Ghana** (f)	['gana]
Great Britain	**Marea Britanie** (f)	['marʲa bri'tanie]
Greece	**Grecia** (f)	['gretʃia]
Haiti	**Haiti** (n)	[ha'iti]
Hungary	**Ungaria** (f)	[un'garia]

100. Countries. Part 2

Iceland	**Islanda** (f)	[is'landa]
India	**India** (f)	['india]
Indonesia	**Indonezia** (f)	[indo'nezia]
Iran	**Iran** (n)	[i'ran]
Iraq	**Irak** (n)	[i'rak]
Ireland	**Irlanda** (f)	[ir'landa]
Israel	**Israel** (n)	[isra'el]
Italy	**Italia** (f)	[i'talia]
Jamaica	**Jamaica** (f)	[ʒa'majka]
Japan	**Japonia** (f)	[ʒa'ponia]
Jordan	**Iordania** (f)	[jor'dania]
Kazakhstan	**Kazahstan** (n)	[kazah'stan]
Kenya	**Kenia** (f)	['kenia]
Kirghizia	**Kîrgîzstan** (m)	[kɨrgɨz'stan]
Kuwait	**Kuweit** (n)	[kuve'it]
Laos	**Laos** (n)	['laos]
Latvia	**Letonia** (f)	[le'tonia]
Lebanon	**Liban** (n)	[li'ban]
Libya	**Libia** (f)	['libia]
Liechtenstein	**Liechtenstein** (m)	[lihten'ʃtajn]
Lithuania	**Lituania** (f)	[litu'ania]
Luxembourg	**Luxemburg** (m)	[luksem'burg]
Macedonia (Republic of ~)	**Macedonia** (f)	[matʃe'donia]
Madagascar	**Madagascar** (n)	[madagas'kar]
Malaysia	**Malaezia** (f)	[mala'ezia]
Malta	**Malta** (f)	['malta]
Mexico	**Mexic** (n)	['meksik]
Moldova, Moldavia	**Moldova** (f)	[mol'dova]
Monaco	**Monaco** (m)	[mo'nako]
Mongolia	**Mongolia** (f)	[mon'golia]
Montenegro	**Muntenegru** (m)	[munte'negru]
Morocco	**Maroc** (n)	[ma'rok]
Myanmar	**Myanmar** (m)	[mjan'mar]
Namibia	**Namibia** (f)	[na'mibia]
Nepal	**Nepal** (n)	[ne'pal]
Netherlands	**Ţările de Jos** (f pl)	['tserile de ʒos]
New Zealand	**Noua Zeelandă** (f)	['nowa zee'landə]
North Korea	**Coreea** (f) **de Nord**	[ko'rea de 'nord]
Norway	**Norvegia** (f)	[nor'veʤia]

101. Countries. Part 3

Pakistan	**Pakistan** (n)	[paki'stan]
Palestine	**Palestina** (f)	[pales'tina]

Panama	Panama (f)	[pana'ma]
Paraguay	Paraguay (n)	[paragu'aj]
Peru	Peru (n)	['peru]
Poland	Polonia (f)	[po'lonia]
Portugal	Portugalia (f)	[portu'galia]
Romania	România (f)	[rominia]
Russia	Rusia (f)	['rusia]

Saudi Arabia	Arabia (f) Saudită	[a'rabia sau'ditə]
Scotland	Scoţia (f)	['skotsia]
Senegal	Senegal (n)	[sene'gal]
Serbia	Serbia (f)	['serbija]
Slovakia	Slovacia (f)	[slo'vatʃia]
Slovenia	Slovenia (f)	[slo'venia]

South Africa	Africa de Sud (f)	['afrika de sud]
South Korea	Coreea (f) de Sud	[ko'rea de 'sud]
Spain	Spania (f)	['spania]
Suriname	Surinam (n)	[suri'nam]
Sweden	Suedia (f)	[su'edia]
Switzerland	Elveţia (f)	[el'vetsia]
Syria	Siria (f)	['sirija]

Taiwan	Taiwan (m)	[taj'van]
Tajikistan	Tadjikistan (m)	[tadʒiki'stan]
Tanzania	Tanzania (f)	[tan'zania]
Tasmania	Tasmania (f)	[tas'mania]
Thailand	Thailanda (f)	[taj'landa]
Tunisia	Tunisia (f)	[tu'nisia]
Turkey	Turcia (f)	['turtʃia]
Turkmenistan	Turkmenistan (n)	[turkmeni'stan]

Ukraine	Ucraina (f)	[ukra'ina]
United Arab Emirates	Emiratele (n pl) Arabe Unite	[emi'ratele a'rabe u'nite]
United States of America	Statele (n pl) Unite ale Americii	['statele u'nite 'ale a'meritʃij]
Uruguay	Uruguay (n)	[urugu'aj]
Uzbekistan	Uzbekistan (n)	[uzbeki'stan]

Vatican	Vatican (m)	[vati'kan]
Venezuela	Venezuela (f)	[venezu'ela]
Vietnam	Vietnam (n)	[viet'nam]
Zanzibar	Zanzibar (n)	[zanzi'bar]

GASTRONOMIC GLOSSARY

This section contains a lot of
words and terms associated
with food. This dictionary will
make it easier for you to
understand the menu at a
restaurant and choose
the right dish

T&P Books Publishing

English-Romanian gastronomic glossary

aftertaste	aromă (f)	[a'romə]
almond	migdală (f)	[mig'dalə]
anise	anason (m)	[ana'son]
aperitif	aperitiv (n)	[aperi'tiv]
appetite	poftă (f) de mâncare	['poftə de mɨ'nkare]
appetizer	gustare (f)	[gus'tare]
apple	măr (n)	[mər]
apricot	caisă (f)	[ka'isə]
artichoke	anghinare (f)	[angi'nare]
asparagus	sparanghel (m)	[sparan'gel]
Atlantic salmon	somon (m)	[so'mon]
avocado	avocado (n)	[avo'kado]
bacon	costiță (f) afumată	[kos'titsə afu'matə]
banana	banană (f)	[ba'nanə]
barley	orz (n)	[orz]
bartender	barman (m)	['barman]
basil	busuioc (n)	[busu'jok]
bay leaf	foi (f) de dafin	[foj de 'dafin]
beans	boabe (f pl)	[bo'abe]
beef	carne (f) de vită	['karne de 'vitə]
beer	bere (f)	['bere]
beet	sfeclă (f)	['sfeklə]
bell pepper	piper (m)	[pi'per]
berries	fructe (n pl) de pădure	['frukte de pə'dure]
berry	boabă (f)	[bo'abə]
bilberry	afină (f)	[a'finə]
birch bolete	pitarcă (f)	[pi'tarkə]
bitter	amar	[a'mar]
black coffee	cafea (f) neagră	[ka'fʲa 'nʲagrə]
black pepper	piper (m) negru	[pi'per 'negru]
black tea	ceai (n) negru	[tʃaj 'negru]
blackberry	mură (f)	['murə]
blackcurrant	coacăză (f) neagră	[ko'akəzə 'nʲagrə]
boiled	fiert	[fiert]
bottle opener	deschizător (n) de sticle	[deskizə'tor de 'stikle]
bread	pâine (f)	['pɨne]
breakfast	micul dejun (n)	['mikul de'ʒun]
bream	plătică (f)	[plə'tikə]
broccoli	broccoli (m)	['brokoli]
Brussels sprouts	varză (f) de Bruxelles	['varzə de bruk'sel]
buckwheat	hrişcă (f)	['hriʃkə]
butter	unt (n)	['unt]
buttercream	cremă (f)	['kremə]
cabbage	varză (f)	['varzə]

cake	prăjitură (f)	[prəʒi'turə]
cake	tort (n)	[tort]
calorie	calorie (f)	[kalo'rie]
can opener	deschizător (n) de conserve	[deskizə'tor de kon'serve]
candy	bomboană (f)	[bombo'anə]
canned food	conserve (f pl)	[kon'serve]
cappuccino	cafea (f) cu frișcă	[ka'fʲa ku 'friʃkə]
caraway	chimen (m)	[ki'men]
carbohydrates	hidrați (m pl) de carbon	[hi'dratsʲ de kar'bon]
carbonated	carbogazoasă	[karbogazo'asə]
carp	crap (m)	[krap]
carrot	morcov (m)	['morkov]
catfish	somn (m)	[somn]
cauliflower	conopidă (f)	[kono'pidə]
caviar	icre (f pl) de pește	['ikre de 'peʃte]
celery	țelină (f)	['tselinə]
cep	hrib (m)	[hrib]
cereal crops	cereale (f pl)	[tʃere'ale]
champagne	șampanie (f)	[ʃam'panie]
chanterelle	gălbior (m)	[gəlbi'or]
check	notă (f) de plată	['notə de 'platə]
cheese	cașcaval (n)	['brinzə]
chewing gum	gumă (f) de mestecat	['gumə de meste'kat]
chicken	carne (f) de găină	['karne de gə'inə]
chocolate	ciocolată (f)	[tʃoko'latə]
chocolate	de, din ciocolată	[de, din tʃoko'latə]
cinnamon	scorțișoară (f)	[skortsiʃo'arə]
clear soup	supă (f) de carne	['supə de 'karne]
cloves	cuișoare (f pl)	[kuiʃo'are]
cocktail	cocteil (n)	[kok'tejl]
coconut	nucă (f) de cocos	['nukə de 'kokos]
cod	batog (m)	[ba'tog]
coffee	cafea (f)	[ka'fʲa]
coffee with milk	cafea (f) cu lapte	[ka'fʲa ku 'lapte]
cognac	coniac (n)	[ko'njak]
cold	rece	['retʃe]
condensed milk	lapte (n) condensat	['lapte konden'sat]
condiment	condiment (n)	[kondi'ment]
confectionery	produse (n pl) de cofetărie	[pro'duse də kofetə'rie]
cookies	biscuit (m)	[bisku'it]
coriander	coriandru (m)	[kori'andru]
corkscrew	tirbușon (n)	[tirbu'ʃon]
corn	porumb (m)	[po'rumb]
corn	porumb (m)	[po'rumb]
cornflakes	fulgi (m pl) de porumb	['fuldʒʲ de po'rumb]
course, dish	fel (n) de mâncare	[fel de mi'nkare]
cowberry	merișor (m)	[meri'ʃor]
crab	crab (m)	[krab]
cranberry	răchițele (f pl)	[rəki'tsele]
cream	frișcă (f)	['friʃkə]

crumb	firimitură (f)	[firimi'turə]
cucumber	castravete (m)	[kastra'vete]
cuisine	bucătărie (f)	[bukətə'rie]
cup	ceaşcă (f)	['ʧaʃkə]
dark beer	bere (f) brună	['bere 'brunə]
date	curmală (f)	[kur'male]
death cap	ciupercă (f) otrăvitoare	[ʧiu'perkə otrəvito'are]
dessert	desert (n)	[de'sert]
diet	dietă (f)	[di'etə]
dill	mărar (m)	[mə'rar]
dinner	cină (f)	['ʧinə]
dried	uscat	[us'kat]
drinking water	apă (f) potabilă	['apə po'tabilə]
duck	carne (f) de raţă	['karne de 'ratsə]
ear	spic (n)	[spik]
edible mushroom	ciupercă (f) comestibilă	[ʧiu'perkə komes'tibilə]
eel	ţipar (m)	[tsi'par]
egg	ou (n)	['ow]
egg white	albuş (n)	[al'buʃ]
egg yolk	gălbenuş	[gəlbe'nuʃ]
eggplant	pătlăgea (f) vânătă	[pətlə'ʤ'a 'vinətə]
eggs	ouă (n pl)	['owə]
Enjoy your meal!	Poftă bună!	['poftə 'bunə]
fats	grăsimi (f pl)	[grə'simi]
fig	smochină (f)	[smo'kinə]
filling	umplutură (f)	[umplu'turə]
fish	peşte (m)	['peʃte]
flatfish	cambulă (f)	[kam'bulə]
flour	făină (f)	[fə'inə]
fly agaric	burete (m) pestriţ	[bu'rete pes'trits]
food	mâncare (f)	[min'kare]
fork	furculiţă (f)	[furku'litsə]
freshly squeezed juice	suc (n) natural	[suk natu'ral]
fried	prăjit	[prə'ʒit]
fried eggs	omletă (f)	[om'letə]
frozen	congelat	[konʤe'lat]
fruit	fruct (n)	[frukt]
fruits	fructe (n pl)	[frukte]
game	vânat (n)	[vi'nat]
gammon	pulpă (f)	['pulpə]
garlic	usturoi (m)	[ustu'roj]
gin	gin (n)	[ʤin]
ginger	ghimber (m)	[gim'ber]
glass	pahar (n)	[pa'har]
glass	cupă (f)	['kupə]
goose	carne (f) de gâscă	['karne de 'giskə]
gooseberry	agrişă (f)	[a'griʃə]
grain	grăunţe (n pl)	[grə'untse]
grape	struguri (m pl)	['strugur']
grapefruit	grepfrut (n)	['grepfrut]
green tea	ceai (n) verde	[ʧaj 'verde]
greens	verdeaţă (f)	[ver'd'atsə]

groats	crupe (f pl)	['krupe]
halibut	calcan (m)	[kal'kan]
ham	şuncă (f)	['ʃunkə]
hamburger	carne (f) tocată	['karne to'katə]
hamburger	hamburger (m)	['hamburger]
hazelnut	alună (f) de pădure	[a'lunə de pə'dure]
herring	scrumbie (f)	[skrum'bie]
honey	miere (f)	['mjere]
horseradish	hrean (n)	[hrʲan]
hot	fierbinte	[fier'binte]
ice	gheaţă (f)	['gʲatsə]
ice-cream	îngheţată (f)	[inge'tsatə]
instant coffee	cafea (f) solubilă	[ka'fʲa so'lubilə]
jam	gem (n)	[dʒem]
jam	dulceaţă (f)	[dul'tʃatsə]
juice	suc (n)	[suk]
kidney bean	fasole (f)	[fa'sole]
kiwi	kiwi (n)	['kivi]
knife	cuţit (n)	[ku'tsit]
lamb	carne (f) de berbec	['karne de ber'bek]
lemon	lămâie (f)	[lə'mie]
lemonade	limonadă (f)	[limo'nadə]
lentil	linte (n)	['linte]
lettuce	salată (f)	[sa'latə]
light beer	bere (f) blondă	['bere 'blondə]
liqueur	lichior (n)	[li'kʲor]
liquors	băuturi (f pl) alcoolice	[bəu'turʲ alko'olitʃe]
liver	ficat (m)	[fi'kat]
lunch	prânz (n)	[prinz]
mackerel	macrou (n)	[ma'krou]
mandarin	mandarină (f)	[manda'rinə]
mango	mango (n)	['mango]
margarine	margarină (f)	[marga'rinə]
marmalade	marmeladă (f)	[marme'ladə]
mashed potatoes	piure (n) de cartofi	[pju're de kar'tofʲ]
mayonnaise	maioneză (f)	[majo'nezə]
meat	carne (f)	['karne]
melon	pepene (m) galben	['pepene 'galben]
menu	meniu (n)	[me'nju]
milk	lapte (n)	['lapte]
milkshake	cocteil (n) din lapte	[kok'tejl din 'lapte]
millet	mei (m)	[mej]
mineral water	apă (f) minerală	['apə mine'ralə]
morel	zbârciog (m)	[zbir'tʃog]
mushroom	ciupercă (f)	[tʃiu'perkə]
mustard	muştar (m)	[muʃ'tar]
non-alcoholic	fără alcool	['fərə alko'ol]
noodles	tăiţei (m)	[təi'tsej]
oats	ovăz (n)	[ovəz]
olive oil	ulei (n) de măsline	[u'lej de məs'line]
olives	olive (f pl)	[o'live]
omelet	omletă (f)	[om'letə]

onion	ceapă (f)	['ʧapə]
orange	portocală (f)	[porto'kalə]
orange juice	suc (n) de portocale	[suk de porto'kale]
orange-cap boletus	pitărcuță (f)	[pitər'kuʦe]
oyster	stridie (f)	['stridie]
pâté	pateu (n)	[pa'teu]
papaya	papaia (f)	[pa'paja]
paprika	paprică (f)	['paprikə]
parsley	pătrunjel (m)	[pətrun'ʒel]
pasta	paste (f pl)	['paste]
pea	mazăre (f)	['mazəre]
peach	piersică (f)	['pjersikə]
peanut	arahidă (f)	[ara'hidə]
pear	pară (f)	['parə]
peel	coajă (f)	[ko'aʒə]
perch	biban (m)	[bi'ban]
pickled	marinat	[mari'nat]
pie	plăcintă (f)	[plə'ʧintə]
piece	bucată (f)	[bu'katə]
pike	ştiucă (f)	['ʃtjukə]
pike perch	şalău (m)	[ʃa'ləu]
pineapple	ananas (m)	[ana'nas]
pistachios	fistic (m)	['fistik]
pizza	pizza (f)	['piʦa]
plate	farfurie (f)	[farfu'rie]
plum	prună (f)	['prunə]
poisonous mushroom	ciupercă (f) otrăvitoare	[ʧiu'perkə otrəvito'are]
pomegranate	rodie (f)	['rodie]
pork	carne (f) de porc	['karne de pork]
porridge	caşă (f)	['kaʃə]
portion	porţie (f)	['portsie]
potato	cartof (m)	[kar'tof]
proteins	proteine (f pl)	[prote'ine]
pub, bar	bar (n)	[bar]
pumpkin	dovleac (m)	[dov'l'ak]
rabbit	carne (f) de iepure de casă	['karne de 'epure de 'kasə]
radish	ridiche (f)	[ri'dike]
raisin	stafidă (f)	[sta'fidə]
raspberry	zmeură (f)	['zmeurə]
recipe	reţetă (f)	[re'tsetə]
red pepper	piper (m) roşu	[pi'per 'roʃu]
red wine	vin (n) roşu	[vin 'roʃu]
redcurrant	coacăză (f) roşie	[ko'akəzə 'roʃie]
refreshing drink	băutură (f) răcoritoare	[bəu'turə rəkorito'are]
rice	orez (n)	[o'rez]
rum	rom (n)	[rom]
russula	vineţică (f)	[vine'ʦikə]
rye	secară (f)	[se'karə]
saffron	şofran (m)	[ʃo'fran]
salad	salată (f)	[sa'latə]
salmon	somon (m)	[so'mon]

salt	sare (f)	['sare]
salty	sărat	[sə'rat]
sandwich	tartină (f)	[tar'tinə]
sardine	sardea (f)	[sar'dʲa]
sauce	sos (n)	[sos]
saucer	farfurioară (f)	[farfurio'arə]
sausage	salam (n)	[sa'lam]
seafood	produse (n pl) marine	[pro'duse ma'rine]
sesame	susan (m)	[su'san]
shark	rechin (m)	[re'kin]
shrimp	crevetă (f)	[kre'vetə]
side dish	garnitură (f)	[garni'turə]
slice	felie (f)	[fe'lie]
smoked	afumat	[afu'mat]
soft drink	băutură (f) fără alcool	[bəu'ture fərə alko'ol]
soup	supă (f)	['supə]
soup spoon	lingură (f)	['lingurə]
sour cherry	vişină (f)	['viʃinə]
sour cream	smântână (f)	[smɨn'tɨnə]
soy	soia (f)	['soja]
spaghetti	spaghete (f pl)	[spa'gete]
sparkling	gazoasă	[gazo'asə]
spice	condiment (n)	[kondi'ment]
spinach	spanac (n)	[spa'nak]
spiny lobster	langustă (f)	[lan'gustə]
spoon	lingură (f)	['lingurə]
squid	calmar (m)	[kal'mar]
steak	biftec (n)	[bif'tek]
still	necarbogazoasă	[nekarbogazo'asə]
strawberry	căpşună (f)	[kəp'ʃunə]
sturgeon	carne (f) de nisetru	['karne de ni'setru]
sugar	zahăr (n)	['zahər]
sunflower oil	ulei (n) de floarea-soarelui	[u'lej de flo'arʲa so'areluj]
sweet	dulce	['dultʃe]
sweet cherry	cireaşă (f)	[tʃi'rʲaʃə]
taste, flavor	gust (n)	[gust]
tasty	gustos	[gus'tos]
tea	ceai (n)	[tʃaj]
teaspoon	linguriţă (f) de ceai	[lingu'ritsə de tʃaj]
tip	bacşiş (n)	[bak'ʃiʃ]
tomato	roşie (f)	['roʃie]
tomato juice	suc (n) de roşii	[suk de 'roʃij]
tongue	limbă (f)	['limbə]
toothpick	scobitoare (f)	[skobito'are]
trout	păstrăv (m)	[pəs'trəv]
tuna	ton (m)	[ton]
turkey	carne (f) de curcan	['karne de 'kurkan]
turnip	nap (m)	[nap]
veal	carne (f) de viţel	['karne de vi'tsel]
vegetable oil	ulei (n) vegetal	[u'lej vedʒe'tal]
vegetables	legume (f pl)	[le'gume]

vegetarian	**vegetarian** (m)	[vedʒetari'an]
vegetarian	**vegetarian**	[vedʒetari'an]
vermouth	**vermut** (n)	[ver'mut]
vienna sausage	**crenvurşt** (n)	[kren'vurʃt]
vinegar	**oţet** (n)	[o'tset]
vitamin	**vitamină** (f)	[vita'minə]
vodka	**votcă** (f)	['votkə]
wafers	**napolitane** (f pl)	[napoli'tane]
waiter	**chelner** (m)	['kelner]
waitress	**chelneriţă** (f)	[kelne'ritsə]
walnut	**nucă** (f)	['nukə]
water	**apă** (f)	['apə]
watermelon	**pepene** (m) **verde**	['pepene 'verde]
wheat	**grâu** (n)	['grɨu]
whiskey	**whisky** (n)	['wiski]
white wine	**vin** (n) **alb**	[vin alb]
wild strawberry	**frag** (m)	[frag]
wine	**vin** (n)	[vin]
wine list	**meniu** (n) **de vinuri**	[menju de 'vinurʲ]
with ice	**cu gheaţă**	[ku 'gʲatsə]
yogurt	**iaurt** (n)	[ja'urt]
zucchini	**dovlecel** (m)	[dovle'tʃel]

îngheţată (f)	[ɨnge'tsatə]	ice-cream
şalău (m)	[ʃa'ləu]	pike perch
şampanie (f)	[ʃam'panie]	champagne
şofran (m)	[ʃo'fran]	saffron
ştiucă (f)	['ʃtjukə]	pike
şuncă (f)	['ʃunkə]	ham
ţelină (f)	['tselinə]	celery
ţipar (m)	[tsi'par]	eel
afină (f)	[a'finə]	bilberry
afumat	[afu'mat]	smoked
agrişă (f)	[a'griʃə]	gooseberry
albuş (n)	[al'buʃ]	egg white
alună (f) de pădure	[a'lunə de pə'dure]	hazelnut
amar	[a'mar]	bitter
ananas (m)	[ana'nas]	pineapple
anason (m)	[ana'son]	anise
anghinare (f)	[angi'nare]	artichoke
apă (f)	['apə]	water
apă (f) minerală	['apə mine'ralə]	mineral water
apă (f) potabilă	['apə po'tabilə]	drinking water
aperitiv (n)	[aperi'tiv]	aperitif
arahidă (f)	[ara'hidə]	peanut
aromă (f)	[a'romə]	aftertaste
avocado (n)	[avo'kado]	avocado
băutură (f) fără alcool	[bəu'turə fərə alko'ol]	soft drink
băutură (f) răcoritoare	[bəu'turə rəkorito'are]	refreshing drink
băuturi (f pl) alcoolice	[bəu'turi alko'olitʃe]	liquors
bacşiş (n)	[bak'ʃiʃ]	tip
banană (f)	[ba'nanə]	banana
bar (n)	[bar]	pub, bar
barman (m)	['barman]	bartender
batog (m)	[ba'tog]	cod
bere (f)	['bere]	beer
bere (f) blondă	['bere 'blondə]	light beer
bere (f) brună	['bere 'brunə]	dark beer
biban (m)	[bi'ban]	perch
biftec (n)	[bif'tek]	steak
biscuit (m)	[bisku'it]	cookies
boabă (f)	[bo'abə]	berry
boabe (f pl)	[bo'abe]	beans
bomboană (f)	[bombo'anə]	candy
broccoli (m)	['brokoli]	broccoli
bucătărie (f)	[bukətə'rie]	cuisine
bucată (f)	[bu'katə]	piece

burete (m) **pestriț**	[bu'rete pes'trits]	fly agaric
busuioc (n)	[busu'jok]	basil
căpşună (f)	[kəp'ʃunə]	strawberry
caşă (f)	['kaʃə]	porridge
caşcaval (n)	['brinzə]	cheese
cafea (f)	[ka'fʲa]	coffee
cafea (f) **cu frişcă**	[ka'fʲa ku 'friʃkə]	cappuccino
cafea (f) **cu lapte**	[ka'fʲa ku 'lapte]	coffee with milk
cafea (f) **neagră**	[ka'fʲa 'nʲagrə]	black coffee
cafea (f) **solubilă**	[ka'fʲa so'lubilə]	instant coffee
caisă (f)	[ka'isə]	apricot
calcan (m)	[kal'kan]	halibut
calmar (m)	[kal'mar]	squid
calorie (f)	[kalo'rie]	calorie
cambulă (f)	[kam'bulə]	flatfish
carbogazoasă	[karbogazo'ase]	carbonated
carne (f)	['karne]	meat
carne (f) **de berbec**	['karne de ber'bek]	lamb
carne (f) **de curcan**	['karne de 'kurkan]	turkey
carne (f) **de gâscă**	['karne de 'giskə]	goose
carne (f) **de găină**	['karne de gə'inə]	chicken
carne (f) **de iepure de casă**	['karne de 'epure de 'kasə]	rabbit
carne (f) **de nisetru**	['karne de ni'setru]	sturgeon
carne (f) **de porc**	['karne de pork]	pork
carne (f) **de rață**	['karne de 'ratsə]	duck
carne (f) **de vițel**	['karne de vi'tsel]	veal
carne (f) **de vită**	['karne de 'vitə]	beef
carne (f) **tocată**	['karne to'katə]	hamburger
cartof (m)	[kar'tof]	potato
castravete (m)	[kastra'vete]	cucumber
ceaşcă (f)	['tʃaʃkə]	cup
ceai (n)	[tʃaj]	tea
ceai (n) **negru**	[tʃaj 'negru]	black tea
ceai (n) **verde**	[tʃaj 'verde]	green tea
ceapă (f)	['tʃapə]	onion
cereale (f pl)	[tʃere'ale]	cereal crops
chelner (m)	['kelner]	waiter
chelneriță (f)	[kelne'ritsə]	waitress
chimen (m)	[ki'men]	caraway
cină (f)	['tʃinə]	dinner
ciocolată (f)	[tʃioko'latə]	chocolate
cireaşă (f)	[tʃi'rʲaʃə]	sweet cherry
ciupercă (f)	[tʃiu'perkə]	mushroom
ciupercă (f) **comestibilă**	[tʃiu'perkə komes'tibilə]	edible mushroom
ciupercă (f) **otrăvitoare**	[tʃiu'perkə otrəvito'are]	poisonous mushroom
ciupercă (f) **otrăvitoare**	[tʃiu'perkə otrəvito'are]	death cap
coacăză (f) **neagră**	[ko'akəzə 'nʲagrə]	blackcurrant
coacăză (f) **roşie**	[ko'akəzə 'roʃie]	redcurrant
coajă (f)	[ko'aʒə]	peel
cocteil (n)	[kok'tejl]	cocktail
cocteil (n) **din lapte**	[kok'tejl din 'lapte]	milkshake

condiment (n)	[kondi'ment]	condiment
condiment (n)	[kondi'ment]	spice
congelat	[kondʒe'lat]	frozen
coniac (n)	[ko'njak]	cognac
conopidă (f)	[kono'pidə]	cauliflower
conserve (f pl)	[kon'serve]	canned food
coriandru (m)	[kori'andru]	coriander
costiță (f) afumată	[kos'titsə afu'matə]	bacon
crab (m)	[krab]	crab
crap (m)	[krap]	carp
cremă (f)	['kremə]	buttercream
crenvurşt (n)	[kren'vurʃt]	vienna sausage
crevetă (f)	[kre'vetə]	shrimp
crupe (f pl)	['krupe]	groats
cu gheaţă	[ku 'gʲatsə]	with ice
cuţit (n)	[ku'tsit]	knife
cuişoare (f pl)	[kuiʃo'are]	cloves
cupă (f)	['kupə]	glass
curmală (f)	[kur'malə]	date
de, din ciocolată	[de, din tʃioko'latə]	chocolate
deschizător (n) de conserve	[deskizə'tor de kon'serve]	can opener
deschizător (n) de sticle	[deskizə'tor de 'stikle]	bottle opener
desert (n)	[de'sert]	dessert
dietă (f)	[di'etə]	diet
dovleac (m)	[dov'lʲak]	pumpkin
dovlecel (m)	[dovle'tʃel]	zucchini
dulce	['dultʃe]	sweet
dulceaţă (f)	[dul'tʃatsə]	jam
făină (f)	[fə'inə]	flour
fără alcool	['fərə alko'ol]	non-alcoholic
farfurie (f)	[farfu'rie]	plate
farfurioară (f)	[farfurio'arə]	saucer
fasole (f)	[fa'sole]	kidney bean
fel (n) de mâncare	[fel de mʲ'nkare]	course, dish
felie (f)	[fe'lie]	slice
ficat (m)	[fi'kat]	liver
fierbinte	[fier'binte]	hot
fiert	[fiert]	boiled
firimitură (f)	[firimi'turə]	crumb
fistic (m)	['fistik]	pistachios
foi (f) de dafin	[foj de 'dafin]	bay leaf
frag (m)	[frag]	wild strawberry
frişcă (f)	['friʃkə]	cream
fruct (n)	[frukt]	fruit
fructe (n pl)	[frukte]	fruits
fructe (n pl) de pădure	['frukte de pə'dure]	berries
fulgi (m pl) de porumb	['fuldʒi de po'rumb]	cornflakes
furculiţă (f)	[furku'litsə]	fork
gălbenuş	[gəlbe'nuʃ]	egg yolk
gălbior (m)	[gəlbi'or]	chanterelle
garnitură (f)	[garni'turə]	side dish

gazoasă	[gazo'asə]	sparkling
gem (n)	[dʒem]	jam
gheață (f)	['gʲatsə]	ice
ghimber (m)	[gim'ber]	ginger
gin (n)	[dʒin]	gin
grâu (n)	['grʲu]	wheat
grăsimi (f pl)	[grə'simʲ]	fats
grăunțe (n pl)	[grə'untse]	grain
grepfrut (n)	['grepfrut]	grapefruit
gumă (f) de mestecat	['gumə de meste'kat]	chewing gum
gust (n)	[gust]	taste, flavor
gustare (f)	[gus'tare]	appetizer
gustos	[gus'tos]	tasty
hamburger (m)	['hamburger]	hamburger
hidrați (m pl) de carbon	[hi'dratsʲ de kar'bon]	carbohydrates
hrean (n)	[hrʲan]	horseradish
hrișcă (f)	['hriʃkə]	buckwheat
hrib (m)	[hrib]	cep
iaurt (n)	[ja'urt]	yogurt
icre (f pl) de pește	['ikre de 'peʃte]	caviar
kiwi (n)	['kivi]	kiwi
lămâie (f)	[lə'mʲe]	lemon
langustă (f)	[lan'gustə]	spiny lobster
lapte (n)	['lapte]	milk
lapte (n) condensat	['lapte konden'sat]	condensed milk
legume (f pl)	[le'gume]	vegetables
lichior (n)	[li'kør]	liqueur
limbă (f)	['limbə]	tongue
limonadă (f)	[limo'nadə]	lemonade
lingură (f)	['lingurə]	spoon
lingură (f)	['lingurə]	soup spoon
linguriță (f) de ceai	[lingu'ritsə de tʃaj]	teaspoon
linte (n)	['linte]	lentil
mâncare (f)	[mɨn'kare]	food
măr (n)	[mər]	apple
mărar (m)	[mə'rar]	dill
macrou (n)	[ma'krou]	mackerel
maioneză (f)	[majo'nezə]	mayonnaise
mandarină (f)	[manda'rinə]	mandarin
mango (n)	['mango]	mango
margarină (f)	[marga'rinə]	margarine
marinat	[mari'nat]	pickled
marmeladă (f)	[marme'ladə]	marmalade
mazăre (f)	['mazəre]	pea
mei (m)	[mej]	millet
meniu (n)	[me'nju]	menu
meniu (n) de vinuri	[menju de 'vinurʲ]	wine list
merișor (m)	[meri'ʃor]	cowberry
micul dejun (n)	['mikul de'ʒun]	breakfast
miere (f)	['mjere]	honey
migdală (f)	[mig'dalə]	almond
morcov (m)	['morkov]	carrot

muştar (m)	[muʃ'tar]	mustard
mură (f)	['murə]	blackberry
nap (m)	[nap]	turnip
napolitane (f pl)	[napoli'tane]	wafers
necarbogazoasă	[nekarbogazo'asə]	still
notă (f) de plată	['notə de 'platə]	check
nucă (f)	['nukə]	walnut
nucă (f) de cocos	['nukə de 'kokos]	coconut
oţet (n)	[o'ʦet]	vinegar
olive (f pl)	[o'live]	olives
omletă (f)	[om'letə]	fried eggs
omletă (f)	[om'letə]	omelet
orez (n)	[o'rez]	rice
orz (n)	[orz]	barley
ou (n)	['ow]	egg
ouă (n pl)	['owə]	eggs
ovăz (n)	[ovəz]	oats
pâine (f)	['pɨne]	bread
păstrăv (m)	[pəs'trəv]	trout
pătlăgea (f) vânătă	[pətlə'ʤʲa 'vɨnətə]	eggplant
pătrunjel (m)	[pətrun'ʒel]	parsley
pahar (n)	[pa'har]	glass
papaia (f)	[pa'paja]	papaya
paprică (f)	['paprikə]	paprika
pară (f)	['parə]	pear
paste (f pl)	['paste]	pasta
pateu (n)	[pa'teu]	pâté
peşte (m)	['peʃte]	fish
pepene (m) galben	['pepene 'galben]	melon
pepene (m) verde	['pepene 'verde]	watermelon
piersică (f)	['pjersikə]	peach
piper (m)	[pi'per]	bell pepper
piper (m) negru	[pi'per 'negru]	black pepper
piper (m) roşu	[pi'per 'roʃu]	red pepper
pitărcuţă (f)	[pitər'kuʦə]	orange-cap boletus
pitarcă (f)	[pi'tarkə]	birch bolete
piure (n) de cartofi	[pju're de kar'tofʲ]	mashed potatoes
pizza (f)	['piʦa]	pizza
plăcintă (f)	[plə'ʧintə]	pie
plătică (f)	[plə'tikə]	bream
poftă (f) de mâncare	['poftə de mɨ'nkare]	appetite
Poftă bună!	['poftə 'bunə]	Enjoy your meal!
porţie (f)	['porʦie]	portion
portocală (f)	[porto'kalə]	orange
porumb (m)	[po'rumb]	corn
porumb (m)	[po'rumb]	corn
prânz (n)	[prɨnz]	lunch
prăjit	[prə'ʒit]	fried
prăjitură (f)	[prəʒi'turə]	cake
produse (n pl) de cofetărie	[pro'duse də kofete'rie]	confectionery
produse (n pl) marine	[pro'duse ma'rine]	seafood

proteine (f pl)	[prote'ine]	proteins
prună (f)	['prunə]	plum
pulpă (f)	['pulpə]	gammon
răchițele (f pl)	[rəki'tsele]	cranberry
rețetă (f)	[re'tsetə]	recipe
rece	['retʃe]	cold
rechin (m)	[re'kin]	shark
ridiche (f)	[ri'dike]	radish
roşie (f)	['roʃie]	tomato
rodie (f)	['rodie]	pomegranate
rom (n)	[rom]	rum
sărat	[sə'rat]	salty
salam (n)	[sa'lam]	sausage
salată (f)	[sa'latə]	lettuce
salată (f)	[sa'latə]	salad
sardea (f)	[sar'dʲa]	sardine
sare (f)	['sare]	salt
scobitoare (f)	[skobito'are]	toothpick
scorțişoară (f)	[skortsiʃo'arə]	cinnamon
scrumbie (f)	[skrum'bie]	herring
secară (f)	[se'karə]	rye
sfeclă (f)	['sfeklə]	beet
smântână (f)	[smɨn'tɨnə]	sour cream
smochină (f)	[smo'kinə]	fig
soia (f)	['soja]	soy
somn (m)	[somn]	catfish
somon (m)	[so'mon]	salmon
somon (m)	[so'mon]	Atlantic salmon
sos (n)	[sos]	sauce
spaghete (f pl)	[spa'gete]	spaghetti
spanac (n)	[spa'nak]	spinach
sparanghel (m)	[sparan'gel]	asparagus
spic (n)	[spik]	ear
stafidă (f)	[sta'fidə]	raisin
stridie (f)	['stridie]	oyster
struguri (m pl)	['strugurʲ]	grape
suc (n)	[suk]	juice
suc (n) de portocale	[suk de porto'kale]	orange juice
suc (n) de roşii	[suk de 'roʃij]	tomato juice
suc (n) natural	[suk natu'ral]	freshly squeezed juice
supă (f)	['supə]	soup
supă (f) de carne	['supə de 'karne]	clear soup
susan (m)	[su'san]	sesame
tăiţei (m)	[təi'tsej]	noodles
tartină (f)	[tar'tinə]	sandwich
tirbuşon (n)	[tirbu'ʃon]	corkscrew
ton (m)	[ton]	tuna
tort (n)	[tort]	cake
ulei (n) de floarea-soarelui	[u'lej de flo'arʲa so'areluj]	sunflower oil
ulei (n) de măsline	[u'lej de məs'line]	olive oil
ulei (n) vegetal	[u'lej vedʒe'tal]	vegetable oil

umplutură (f)	[umplu'turə]	filling
unt (n)	['unt]	butter
uscat	[us'kat]	dried
usturoi (m)	[ustu'roj]	garlic
vânat (n)	[vɨ'nat]	game
varză (f)	['varzə]	cabbage
varză (f) de Bruxelles	['varzə de bruk'sel]	Brussels sprouts
vegetarian	[vedʒetari'an]	vegetarian
vegetarian (m)	[vedʒetari'an]	vegetarian
verdeață (f)	[ver'dʲatsə]	greens
vermut (n)	[ver'mut]	vermouth
vişină (f)	['viʃinə]	sour cherry
vin (n)	[vin]	wine
vin (n) alb	[vin alb]	white wine
vin (n) roşu	[vin 'roʃu]	red wine
vinețică (f)	[vine'tsikə]	russula
vitamină (f)	[vita'minə]	vitamin
votcă (f)	['votkə]	vodka
whisky (n)	['wiski]	whiskey
zahăr (n)	['zahər]	sugar
zbârciog (m)	[zbɨr'tʃiog]	morel
zmeură (f)	['zmeurə]	raspberry

CPSIA information can be obtained
at www.ICGtesting.com
Printed in the USA
BVHW041401270920
589722BV00020B/534